MW00837608

KARMANN GHIA

KARMANN GHIA

Stuart Johnston

First published in Great Britain in 1995
by Osprey, an imprint of Reed Consumer
Books Limited, Michelin House,
81 Fulham Road, London SW3 6RB and
Auckland, Melbourne, Singapore and Toronto.

© Stuart Johnston 1995

All rights reserved. Apart from any fair
dealing for the purposes of private study,
research, criticism or review, as permitted
under the Copyright, Designs and Patents
Act, 1988, no part of this publication may be
reproduced, stored in a retrieval system, or
transmitted in any form or by any means
electronic, electrical, chemical, mechanical,
optical, photocopying, recording or otherwise,
without prior written permission. All
enquiries should be addressed to the
Publisher.

ISBN 185532 509 8

Project Editor Shaun Barrington
Editor Simon McAuslane
Page design Paul Kime/Ward Peacock
Partnership

Printed in Hong Kong

**All photographs by Stuart Johnston
except pages 2, 5, 7, 74, 88 and 110
by Colin Burnham. With grateful
thanks to all the owners who gave
up their time and surrendered their
beautiful machinery to the critical
gaze of the lens.**

For a catalogue of all books published by Osprey Automotive
please write to:

**The Marketing Department, Reed Consumer Books,
1st Floor, Michelin House, 81 Fulham Road, London SW3 6RB**

Contents

Even as a dragster the Ghia shape retains a certain delicacy of line

Karmann Sense

I was halfway towards somewhere in the desert when I began to get a sense of what I had beneath me, on a scorching November day in that part of the country known as the Karoo. A vast expanse of emptiness where temperatures of 40 degrees Celcius are dealt with by simply wearing a khaki hat. Where it is so quiet you eventually slow your thinking down to the point where thought stops. And there you are.

The 1966 Karmann tootling along according to my throttle foot had developed an easy, loping gait that saw it maintain a cruising speed of 110 km/h with no apparent strain. A big change in perception from when I had taken delivery of the little aquamarine and white car two nights before and battled up the hilly inclines of Johannesburg's suburbs with taxis, BMWs, Mercedes and Nissan turbos hooting me even further onto the verge.

I had ignored the advice of countless magazine articles. The ones jerked from the editor's musty pile of stand-bys, with titles like "How to buy a Banger for Five Hundred Bucks". I had practically bought a car over the telephone from someone I didn't know, 1400 km from where I lived. Compounding my sin by being in an emotional state of excitement when I finally found the obscure address, I viewed the car at night. I then clumsily tried to beat the owner down by about 5 per cent of his rather steep asking price and then capitulated immediately. I signed on the dotted line after a mere 2 km drive, in darkness over strange roads. And now, with over 500 km of a 1400 km drive still ahead, I was starting to become convinced that the twenty four-year-old coupe would actually make Cape Town.

The thing is, when it comes to Karmann Ghias (I was discovering almost without wanting to) logic and other left-brain functioning is put on the back-burner. Like all great cars, the Karmann Ghia is first and foremost a communicator, and I was learning to tune into those subtle rhythms wrought by a remarkable synthesis of great automotive imagination and craftsmanship.

Right
Cruising along in the desert at a steady 65

There is the body, of course, that seduces you by its shape, voluptuous in its curves yet petite in its comparative dimensions. There is the workmanship, which sees door handles, dashboard knobs, fender shapes and light fittings still new-looking after years of service. There is the steering, which is intrinsically communicative, and the road-holding, which is genuinely in the sports car class, despite being Beetle-based and thus oversteer-prone. The legendary Volkswagen gearchange is wonderful in its precision, although its spring-loading takes some acclimatisation. And then, there is the engine.

The four cylinder Boxer motor is still the biggest stumbling block that Ghia freaks encounter when enthusing about their ponies (I considered using "steeds" but the imagery is perhaps a little too presumptuous for a car which was launched with just 30 horsepower). The problem is that in the minds of countless students, ageing hippies, housewives, bank clerks – and just about everyone else – the Volkswagen engine, identical to

Above
Long trips require extra luggage space – of course this classic deck carrier doesn't hurt the lines of the car either

Left
Original colour schemes were chosen with as much care as the Ghia stylists took, working on the drawing boards in the early '50s. The resultant harmony is there for all owners and enthusiasts to enjoy

Four decades on, the flowing lines of the Volkswagen Karmann Ghia are again contemporary with the offerings from Honda, Ford and Mazda, among others, who are approaching the symmetry of the Type 1 coupé

those found in common and vegetable patch Beetles the world over, has never been associated with sports car charisma.

So here we have a car that looks as if it could have won the Mille Miglia in 1955, nevertheless making piffling wheezing noises out of the same twin pea-shooter pipes found on the People's Wagon. And by 1990s standards, it's slow. In fact even in 1956, when the first road tests began to appear in motoring publications, speed was not considered an appropriate yardstick with which to judge the the Karmann Ghia.

Rationalising the engine as reliable, simple to maintain, with clockwork starting habits, is okay when you are doing your monthly household budget. But for those late nights at the bar, when trying to top the insurance salesman's tale about his duel with a Toyota Supra over the pass, you don't really want to start talking fuel consumption and spares availability.

The bodywork was hand-crafted on the Karmann Ghia, and the nose section was welded together from numerous plates before being hand-ground and filled

At times like this, it is essential that you have at least one long drive with a Karmann under your belt. Preferably in the desert. Alone. Here the subtle rhythms of that warbling air-cooled motor will reveal themselves. How a change of throttle alters the harmonics of the motor behind you, even though the revs don't seem to change. How temperature is critical to the performance of what some have described as a 'fan driven' engine. How to judge the precise moment for a gearchange, before the engine begins to over rev or to lug.

This ever-changing nature of the horizontally-opposed four cylinder can probably be explained by technical analysis. The relative state of flux of the engine casings, wrought as they are, of magnesium. The reliance on fresh air, fan-forced over and between the cooling fins of the alloy cylinder heads and cast iron barrels to keep engine temperatures to tolerable levels. The use of a simple vacuum advance distributor and a contact-breaker system for ignition. You can think about all this as you drive a Ghia. Most importantly, now that most drivers are cocooned, separated from their powerplants, a Ghia requires you to tune in, and listen.

With a straight road ahead, out in the desert, I started to notice the welcoming smiles of passing motorists in their '90s jelly-bean cars, appreciating the lines of what has become a true, yet most affordable classic. I, in my turn, gazed out around me through the glass that is curved in all six portals and which, with mere slivers for roof posts, offers a remarkably clear view through 360°.

The teardrop-shaped side windows impart a delicious aura of opulence from within, as if you are on the way to the opera in a 1930 Figoni-bodied Delahaye. You sit way, way down, close to the tar, and yet you don't feel oppressed as you do in a mid-engined Ferrari. The gauges are so stark in their simplicity yet impart a touch of Art Deco to the cabin. Nothing about the car is mass-produced, despite its humble chassis and drivetrain. And, apart from the road ahead, not a straight line in sight.

The Porsche Connection

There are marque chauvinists that wouldn't be seen dead in a Karmann Ghia because its history is not intertwined with nobility, romance and Swiss bank accounts. This chapter is not for them. For the Ghia converted, I hope that a meander through a surprisingly complex historical maze will lead to the enrichening realisation that the Ghia's charm extends way beneath its sultry exterior.

By the time the "Beetle in an Italian Sports Jacket" was mooted by Heinz Nordhoff in 1951, Germany's post-war industrial renaissance was

Below
A 1000 cc 'boxer' motor, good for 100 km/h (62 mph) and torsion bar suspension were the principal Porsche design themes carried through on production Beetles. Note the lack of a rear window!

Right

A post-war Beetle, with the famous (now highly desirable) split rear window. Note the large VW logos on the hubcaps, which identify the car as a late 1940s model

well underway. As General Manager of Volkswagen AG from 1948 onwards, Nordhoff was gradually coming under pressure to introduce a new-shaped People's Car as the average German enjoyed increasing affluence.

This was hardly surprising, as the original Beetle concept dated back to 1932, a time when the future Fuhrer was mesmerising countless Germans with various visions, including one where everyone could and would own a motorcar.

The Father of The Beetle was not Adolf Hitler, as many people suppose, but Ferdinand Porsche, who remains one of the most influential automotive designers of all time. Prior to his air-cooled boxer design, Dr Porsche was credited with the creation of radical aircraft engines and such automotive classics as the Mercedes-Benz SS and SSK models, and in 1934 he would design the astounding Auto Union V16 Grand Prix cars, which would produce some 550 horsepower, much to Adolf Hitler's delight. However, before the Czech-born Porsche met Hitler he had been working on a flat four cylinder, air-cooled engine, to be accommodated by a torsion bar suspension design system that he had recently patented. (That famous design was to become exclusive to Volkswagen until the patent ran out in 1950).

Motorcycle company NSU had commissioned the fledgling Porsche design studio to produce a lightweight car, a project that Porsche had entertained for some time. Having previously been employed by Daimler-

Benz and Austro Daimler to design massive cars for the German aristocracy, Porsche relished the opportunity to design an everyday vehicle. In fact he had embarked on a similar mission for NSU earlier in the year, using an air-cooled five cylinder radial engine; but owing to the astonishing political and social upheavals taking place in Germany at that time, both projects were destined to be still-born.

Hitler was introduced to Porsche in late 1933 by another significant mover in the German automobile industry, Baron von Oertzen. Although Porsche was patently apolitical, his views on cars and the role they should play in the lives of ordinary people were certainly in sympathy with Hitler's own.

The Ghia's Great Uncle? This Beetle 'streamliner' was built by Ferdinand Porsche in 1939 to take part in the Berlin-Rome-Berlin marathon, which was cancelled with the outbreak of World War II. There is a Ghia-like rear side window and a similar overall 'flow' to the lower half of the car

The Karmann connection with Volkswagen AG came about when the Osnabruck firm, respected coach-builders before the advent of the automobile, began producing cabriolet versions of the Beetle in 1949. Into the 1980s Karmann were still producing topless Beetles!

Having already done most of the groundwork in his aborted projects for Zundapp and NSU it was not difficult for Porsche to present Hitler with a plan for what would become the Beetle. Apart from some details, such as a tubular chassis instead of the ribbed sheetmetal floorpan with a pressed centre tunnel, the initial basic design themes were used to produce a car that would transform the world's motor industry, and remain in production in some corner of the world for over half a century!

By the time the war broke out, Hitler's SS staffers had tested thirty examples of the basic Beetle for a combined distance of two million kilometres. These cars had a 985 cc version of the flat four and looked very Beetle-like, except for the fact that they had no rear screen. There were so few cars on the roads at that time, that rearward vision wasn't really considered essential. In fact, even today, there are many motorists who seem to subscribe to this philosophy!

The famous split window rear screen in fact made its debut just before the war, when 44 cars were produced with this 'styling update' at the new factory-for-the-people, situated just east of Hanover, at Wolfsburg.

At this stage the car was not known as a Volkswagen, but as the KdF-Wagen. KdF stands for *Kraft durch Freude*, which in English translates as 'Strength through Joy'. It was the mantra of Hitler's state run labour organising movement, which held out the promise of prosperity for all – who qualified as Aryan – and a KdF saving stamps scheme was evolved to dock a small amount off each worker's pay. The idea was that eventually, every hard-working German would own the car of his dreams. Or at least a Beetle.

This particular Hitlerian dream, while it did not turn into the kind of nightmare the others did, was just as false. The average worker never did get to amass enough stamps to become mobile. Only 650 'proper' Beetles with saloon bodywork were produced in the new factory once war had been declared in late 1939, as Hitler's men needed the factory to produce military transport and aircraft materials. These Beetle saloons were mainly used by high ranking officers in Hitler's army during the war, but the basic Beetle platform was soon utilised for Military purposes.

The famous Kubelwagen Jeep and amphibious Schwimmwagen troop carrier were built at Wolsfburg, using Beetle floorpans, engines and transmissions, although the latter were modified for increased ground clearance by the addition of a special reduction gear transmission.

A considerable part of the gigantic Wolfsburg factory survived Allied bombing during the war, and initial peacetime agreements saw three key

Early press release shot of a 1955 Ghia. Interesting features of pre-1960 models are the aluminium wheel 'beauty' trims, fixed rear passenger windows and small fresh-air 'nostrils' in the nose

Above

The top's down and the weather is fine. Volkswagen launched the cabriolet version of the Ghia in August 1957, for the 1958 model year. This one, though, is a 1960 version, denoted by its larger 'nostrils' and other detail styling changes

Overleaf

The early coupés used a 30 hp 1192 cc engine which today is commonly known as an 1100 motor. Nevertheless the sleek shape made a top speed of 72 mph possible

British military men, Colonel C.R. Radcliffe, Major Ivan Kirst, and Wing Commander Dick Berryman take over the rebuilding of the establishment. The rationale behind this was two-fold; to provide work for the impoverished citizens of the area, but also because the Allied occupying troops desperately needed transport.

The Wolfsburg Motor Works, as the British called it, was rebuilt with work starting in 1945, and the first full-scale production of Beetles commenced, just a few months after Hitler had committed suicide. By early 1946 an ambitious target set by Radcliffe of 1000 cars a month was being met, despite the obvious logistical difficulties; with workers, for example, having to tack together roof panels out of three different thicknesses of sheetmetal.

As production engineer in charge of 450 workers, Berryman had a simple brief from Radcliffe: "Get Volkswagenwerk working again at all

costs". How Berryman achieved this, from a tangled mess of a factory and workers who were half-starved, is a story all on its own.

Thanks to the Wing Commander's relish of a challenge, that first target of 1000 cars by March 1946 was met, and by year's end some 8000 Beetles had been produced, almost all of these cars being supplied to the Allied occupying personnel. Conditions in the plant were said to be terrible initially, with workers having to contend with icy, ankle-deep water caused by damaged pipes, but the will to succeed was amazing.

The following year Beetles began to appear in German showrooms for the first time. It was Ivan Hirst who appointed the man who would steer Volkswagen to the number one manufacturing spot in Europe, one Heinz Nordhoff. A former manager at Opel before the war, Nordhoff would go on to run the Wolfsburg operation for 20 years and by the end of 1948, nearly 15000 Germans were Beetle-mobile.

A remarkably expansive personality, Nordhoff set his sights on the world export market, and as the Wolfsburg workforce grew to over 10,000 by 1950, the American market was already seen as the prime target. From a slow start of just 390 units sold Stateside that first year, by 1955, the year of the Karmann Ghia's world premier, 36,000 Beetles were sold to Americans. When one considers that this was the start of the Fins, Flash and a Backyard-for-your-Boot era in American automobile design, the achievement by Nordhoff and his team is almost unbelievable.

Dr Ferdinand Porsche had died in 1951, probably as the result of ill-health triggered during his post-war imprisonment in a French jail for his 'assistance' in the Nazi war effort. Most people who knew Porsche Senior were adamant that he had no interest in nationalism or politics, and it could be argued that his fanatical quest to design ever-more innovative machinery would have left little time or energy for any political leanings.

Rightly or wrongly, however, he had greatly assisted the Nazi war machine by designing two of the most powerful tanks of that campaign, as well as supplying the inspiration for the Beetle-based Kubelwagen, of which just fewer than 50,000 were built.

Nevertheless, Porsche had lived to see the Beetle take off like a bat out of hell, at least in sales terms if not in the manner it left the stoplights. The royalties that were his due on each and every Volkswagen sold enabled his son, Ferry, to establish the firm that today bears the awesome Porsche name.

Left
It's difficult to choose between a coupé and a cabriolet in terms of beauty. This '58 cabrio runs widened Type 2 (Kombi) wheels

Ghia for the Nice Age

Germany's post-war commitment to industry was total and totally successful, and in 1955, to the astonishment of anyone connected to the auto industry, the millionth Beetle was produced. What better time than this to celebrate with one of the prettiest bodyshapes of all time and tack it onto a Beetle? Naturally it wasn't so simple, and there were many intense meetings between the three major players in the Karmann Ghia development game.

Wilhelm Karmann GmbH has its headquarters in Osnabruck, near Hanover and although it took the Volkswagen-commissioned coupé to introduce its name to the world, the firm was well-established as a builder of horse-drawn coaches before the dawn of the motorcar. Karmann built its first automobile body in 1902 and in the ensuing decades, after landing major contracts with firms like Opel, it became synonymous with the production of the finest quality convertible bodies.

Karmann first connected to Volkswagen in 1948, after Karosserie Hebmuller was unable to deliver on a promised contract for convertible bodies for the Beetle, or Type 1 as it is officially known. The Karmann Cabriolet differed from the Hebmuller in that it retained the four passenger seating of the Type 1 sedan, whereas the Hebs, as they are affectionately known by collectors today, were two-seaters, with a delightfully symmetrical front-rear relationship.

Despite a rather pram-like arrangement for the hood when folded down, Karmann-built Beetle cabriolets were perennially popular from the late '40s until the 1980s, when production at last gave way to the front-engined, front-wheel drive econobox era already entrenched at VW AG.

With such strong connections being forged with Volkswagen, it was natural that Karmann would be privy to Nordhoff's initial musings over the possibility of a sporty Beetle. Apparently the idea took form as early as 1950, but progress on the scheme was hampered by the difficulty of mating an aesthetically pleasing sporty shape to the Beetle floorpan.

Left
So successful was the styling of the VW Karmann Ghia that arguments developed as to who should take credit for its shape

According to noted automotive historian and technical writer Jan Norbye, who interviewed key staff members of all three concerns for his 1985 publication, *VW Treasures by Karmann*, it was a chance meeting at a European motorshow that saw Wilhelm Karmann Jr communicate to Luigi Segre, owner of the Turin styling house, Carrozzeria Ghia, his ideas on a Volkswagen-based sports car. Dr Karmann tentatively asked Segre to come up with a workable concept and Segre needed no extra encouragement. He took the idea and ran with it. In fact there are claims that he already had such a car on the drawing boards.

Probably the key to the Karmann Ghia's viability lay in the fact that Segre didn't let the floorpan configuration stand in his way. To enable Karmann eventually to build the car, the Osnabruck firm had to modify the standard Beetle chassis by widening the floor pan by 80 mm on each side. The cutaway for the front wheels is also different on the Karmann,

Above
The Karmann Ghia weighed some 120 pounds more than the Beetle of the time, and acceleration was not neck-snapping. But vastly improved aerodynamics gave the car real high-speed cruisability, and the handling was very good for its day. This is a '66 version, with ball-joint front suspension

Left
The balance of proportion achieved by Ghia's Luigi Segre and his team belied the fact that the Karmann-bodied VW was a rear-engined machine

the taper to the steering neck being far more abrupt than the gradual taper of the Beetle chassis.

But these would be production concerns to be tackled at a later date. The stunning shape that he came up with and built as the first full-sized prototype was so good that Karmann had no hesitation in arranging a viewing for top ranking Volkswagen personnel. Once the VW brass were convinced that the car could be produced at an affordable price and still turn a profit, they pinched themselves to make sure this all wasn't a dream. Contracts were drawn up in record time for signing at Wolfsburg, Osnabruck and Turin.

By the end of 1953, the project was underway. Ghia would refine the bodyshape to certain specifications, Volkswagen would supply the chassis and running gear, and Karmann would undertake the building of the body and the final assembly.

Much of Norbye's absorbing account reads like a detective whodunnit, for the simple reason that the Karmann Ghia body shape was so classy, so perfect, that almost every auto stylist in the world would like to take credit for it. Not surprisingly, it has been the subject of controversy ever since.

While Luigi Segre is generally credited with inspiring the design, some Ghia employees at the time say that lesser-known staffers, notably Mario Boano, were in fact responsible for the actual drawings. This was a Ghia in-house matter, but the main grumblings came from across the Atlantic. Apparently Chrysler's design chief at the time, the renowned Virgil Exner, felt that the car looked too much like some of his Chrysler show cars of that era, notably the K-310, and the Chrysler D' Elegance, to be a coincidence. Lending a lot of credence to his case was the fact that Ghia was in fact responsible for building the Chrysler showcars of that period.

Before you dig out your old copies of *Road and Track* and *Motor Trend* and forthrightly condemn Segre, it is a good idea to take a look at a selection of exotically-bodied cars of that period, some of which pre-date the 1952 Chrysler by a good few years. One notable model that springs to mind was the classic Cisitalia of 1950, styled by Pininfarina, which has similar window cutouts to the Karmann Ghia, and also a hint of the bulbous rear fender crease.

Inspiration for the nose treatment on the Ghia can be found in many 1930s designs, mostly of Italian origin. Indeed, by 1948, Ferry Porsche

Right
Achieving a good-looking, well-built cabriolet version of a successful coupé is not always easy, but then Wilhelm Karmann GmbH had been at it since 1901. And Ghia's roots go back to 1915, the Piedmontese master metal worker Giacinto Ghia initially producing custom-built car bodies for wealthy Alfa and Lancia owners

had already produced the prototype of the Porsche 356, and the side windows and nose treatment bear more than a passing resemblance to the Karmann Ghia.

That famous Karmann Ghia rear fender crease, which reportedly was such a bone of contention between the Exner clan and the Segres family, was by no means unique in 1952. In fact, if one studies the rear fenders of the early Studebaker models, of 1948 to 1951 vintage, one can see strong influences of the rear fender line curving into the waistline, which is perhaps where Exner gained his original inspiration for his K310. Exner had, in fact, worked in the studios of Raymond Loewy, the famous designer who created the Coca Cola bottle, and significantly, the Studebaker.

In any event, arguments over the Karmann Ghia's styling inspiration could not have been of too serious a nature, at least at the time of the creation of the prototype. It is significant that Virgil Exner still had his famous show cars built by Ghia until his retirement from Chrysler at the end of the 1950s, and in fact Ghia continued to produce show cars for Chrysler well into the 1960s.

To get the Karmann Ghia into production, the people at Osnabruck had to source hundreds of components from outside suppliers. Contrary to what many non-Ghia owners believe, there is little truth in the conception that the only difference between a Type 1 Karmann Ghia and a Type 1 Volkswagen is in the sheetmetal. Seats, switchgear, wiper mechanisms, gear levers, dashboard knobs, lights, indicators, hood ornaments, bumpers, air cleaners, all the alloy and stainless steel trim, not to mentioned that exquisitely curved glass, is all Karmann-specific (or Ghia dictated, if you prefer).

In light of this, the fact that Karmann were ready to go into production by late 1955 is a remarkable achievement, given the much lengthier gestation periods for cars today. The Frankfurt Show in September was targeted as the public's introduction to the car, but the press was given a preview as early as July 1955. If people think the Ghia's shape is sensational today, one can only imagine the reaction it must have drawn in 1955. What's more, far from being just another show car, here was a two-plus two coupé that the average man could realistically contemplate owning.

Right
Interior styling was elegant, yet simple, in keeping with the car's VW pedigree. However, the first thing a new Ghia owner discovers is that, mechanicals apart, virtually none of the Ghia parts are interchangeable with a Beetle

An Image Statement

An early VW advert for the Ghia revealed that a total of 185 men were involved in the production of one Karmann Ghia body, and those who have ever a tackled a 'down-to-bare metal' restoration on a Ghia will know why.

The workmanship required to produce the endless curves of all the panels was enormous. For instance, the nose is made up of a series of five different panels, welded together and then ground down and filled with pewter. The same goes for almost any part of the body.

Such a labour-intensive project was deemed permissible because the Ghia was viewed mainly as a promotional tool for VW. It is unlikely that management at either Osnabruck or Wolfsburg envisaged a market of more than 500 cars a month for the Ghia. Understandably, it took Karmann GmbH more than a little time to gear up for Ghia production, and in the first three months, until the end of 1955, only 500 cars were actually sold. Thus, there was a waiting list for Karmann Ghias almost from the word go, a situation that would persist pretty much throughout the nineteen-year production span.

Much has been made of the fact that it is the Karmann Ghia's looks that have accounted for its success. While the harmony of that body style – drawn so many decades before the arrival of computer-aided design systems – has always been appreciated by the public at large, it is a mistake to dismiss the mechanicals of the car as irrelevant.

Sure, the Ghia's shape promised Ferrari-like performance, but a top speed of 76 mph was still not to be sneezed at in April 1956, when *Road and Track* tested the car for the first time. Slight re-jetting of the standard 28 mm Solex carb, and the use of a remote airfilter connected to the carb-top by a long metal tube, were the only changes to the standard '1100' Vee Dubs motor plugged into the back. In fact, at this point, we might as well digress for a few paragraphs and clear up some nomenclatural confusion regarding VW air-cooled motors.

Right
Curves everywhere. Curved window glass, Mille-Miglia-like styling and the reliability and servicability of a Volkswagen spelt amazing success for the 'female's favourite'

The '1100' description is in quotes because in fact the motor, as used in Karmann Ghias from the end of 1955 through until 1960, is already a 1200 in terms of its displacement. This had happened in 1954, when displacement was increased from 1131 cc to 1192 cc, while output was pegged at 30 hp (DIN), up five from the 'real' 1100's 25 horses.

More confusion is that in America, this initial, pre-'60 1200 was more often than not known as a 36 horse motor, while in countries where a DIN rating was applied, it was termed a 30 horse unit. It all depended on what horsepower rating you were referring to. Generally, collectors referring to the old '1100' are usually talking about the 30 (DIN) horse motor with the generator pedestal as an integral part of the engine casing. In 1961, the 34 Horse (DIN) motor was introduced. This motor is identified by having the generator pedestal as a separate, bolt-on structure, and is generally known as the 1200 motor.

To get back to the train of thought embarked upon at the start of this chapter, Beetles weren't considered slow cars back in the 1950s, and even in the early 1960s. One has to take into consideration that the average British Morris or Ford Consul very rarely saw a true 70 mph (112 km/h), and that 80 mph for an MG TF was about par for the course in the middle of the decade.

The situation was somewhat different in America, where the great horsepower race had begun with the announcement of Chrysler's Hemi in the early '50s, but still, Ghias weren't considered that much slower than Porsches when they were first launched.

John Bolster, writing in the February 1957 issue of *Autosport*, commented that the Ghia was a "most desirable car" on the open road. While criticising the car for it's "lack of snap" around town, mainly due to the fact that it weighed some 120 pounds more than the contemporary Beetle, Bolster was extremely impressed with the improvements in performance that the aerodynamics of the body had wrought.

Bolster noted that the Karmann Ghia's ability to sustain its top speed as a cruising speed would enable it to "wear down the opposition" of much more powerful cars on long runs, and this is a characteristic that drivers of air-cooled VWs have exploited to their advantage for the past four decades or so.

The now defunct *Auto Age*, a New York-based monthly, tested a red and black Karmann coupé in its April 1956 issue, and waxed lyrical about how "old Miami friends played every variation on the theme of open-mouthed amazement at the beauty of the machine". *Auto Age* recorded a 0-60 mph time for the car of 22 seconds, which is a bit more optimistic than most tests of that era.

However, they also lent the car to the Marquis de Portago, the famous Ferrari racing ace of that period. The Marquis "liked everything about it –

Above right
Women went for the Ghia in a big way in the '50s and they still do. This 1971 cabriolet was recently shipped from Germany to South Africa by its owner

Below right
Many Ghia owners liked to give the impression they were driving a front-engined car, and fake radiator grille intakes were quite popular as a mild customising venture

particularly its suspension and appearance – with two exceptions: closeness of pedals and sluggish middle-gear acceleration."

That sluggishness in mid-gear – as opposed to its relatively impressive top speed – was caused by the additional 120 lbs in bulk. The top end punch, on the other hand, was the result of the much improved drag coefficient of the car. The handling was the result of a much lower centre of gravity than the Beetle, as well as the addition of a front anti-roll bar hooked up to the two king pins. A few years later the Beetle would adapt this as standard.

Apart from the anti-roll bar, the only other modification to the Beetle running gear of note was to soften the angle of the steering column, so that the steering wheel wouldn't stick into the roof lining once the Karmann body was lowered onto the pan. The Ghia still had those controversial swing axles at the rear, which provided great bump absorption, great traction off-road, and were generally fine all round until you started cornering your Volkswagen like a sports car, which is what presumably many Karmann owners would have liked to do.

The imposition of serious lateral forces, of the type generated when you flick your car into a bend just that little bit quicker than the adhesive limits of your car's tyres, could have serious implications on Dr Porsche's rear axle design. The main problem was a camber change from upright, or even a few degrees negative to one so positive that the rear wheels would attempt to tuck themselves under the car as if they were going to bed for the evening. This is where the over-adventurous VW driver often found him or herself. In bed, wondering how it all happened. Actually the Karmann Ghia was not nearly as afflicted by this problem as the top-heavy Beetle saloon, because the car's centre of gravity, with its low overall height and even lower seating position, made it inherently stable. *Auto Age* and *Road and Track* were among a handful of magazines that managed to acquire a Ghia for a few hours of road testing. The demand was such that there were simply none to spare for years to come, and Karmann had to expand its plant to keep up with demand. By the end of 1956, the Osnabruck firm had achieved an amazing total output of 10 000 cars, all of them left-hand-drive coupés.

When August 1957 came around, August being the traditional month for the preview launching of the models for the next model year, the growing number of Ghia fans were in for an even bigger surprise – a stunning convertible version for 1958.

The Karmann top for the Ghia-bodied cabriolets is rated as one of the finest of its kind, with practically no wind leakage. It featured an inner lining as well as padding between the lining and the outer covering which was originally made of canvas or mohair. This is a vinyl top

Vive la Différ

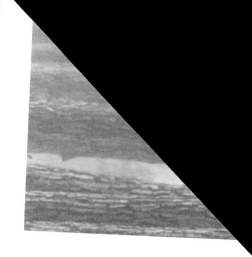

A mistake common to Karmann ro
that all Type 1 Karmann Ghias are
group the Type 3 and the Type 1 t
experience of the Ghia nameplate.

Given that this is a book focussed on the Type 1 Ghia (although the
Type 3 'knife-edge' car is very attractive in its own right), we'll leave
details of the Type 3 out of this chapter, which deals with the astounding
number of variations between the models year by year.

Volkswagen AG issued their own type numbers for the basic Ghia
variations, and these are as follows:

TYPE 143 The original Karmann Ghia coupé, produced between
August 1955 and July 1959. Distinguished by its small fresh air vent
'nostrils' and droop-snout fenders, with the headlights positioned slightly
lower on the bodywork, and small, oblong-shaped tail lights.

TYPE 141 The original Karmann Ghia cabriolet, featuring the same
details as above. Produced between August 1957 and July 1959.

TYPE 144 The 'wide nostril' Karmann coupé. Features much larger
fresh-air vent cutouts in the nose, different front fenders with raised
headlights and reprofiled wheel-arches, the cutouts sweeping back
towards the rear. New, 'leaf-shaped' tail lights. Introduced in August 1959
as a '1960' model, this type number was used through until the end of
production in 1974.

TYPE 142 The cabriolet counterpart of the 144, also featuring the
same nostril, headlight, wheel-arch and tail light changes for the 1960
model year, through until the end. Later detail changes, which will be
listed in this chapter, did not affect the type numbers. While these types
referred to the major changes made, they do not take into account the
detail differences in bumpers, steering wheels, ashtrays, indicator lenses,
headlights, wheels, hubcaps, dashboards, tail lights, glass, trim and
interior made over 19 years of production. While it is possible that there

are other slight changes from model to model, and depending on whether the Ghia in question was produced for export or home market, for left-hand-drive to right-hand drive, the following is a guide for purchasers and restorers, as well as just the dangerously obsessed Ghia devotee.

1956 MODEL YEAR

The first year of production. Chassis numbers on all Karmann Ghias can be found stamped into the floorpan at the rear end of the transmission linkage tunnel. Access to the number is easy, simply by lifting up the rear seat squab. This year's chassis numbers fell between 1060930 and 1394119.

To distinguish this model from other pre-'60 Ghias, the following details are relevant: Only left-hand-drive models were produced during the period August 1955 to July 1959. in the first two model years, the steering wheel is of the standard Beetle type of that era, cream plastic, with two non-dish spokes slightly off-set below the hub and a large black Wolfsburg emblem in the centre. The early model Ghias had no fuel gauge and the accelerator pedal was at this stage still of the roller type, rather than the flat tongue hinged on the floor of later models. The sunvisors were made of plastic and were attached to the rearview mirror housing and thus of the non-swivel type.

The front indicator lenses (turn signals, also referred to by some as park lights) are of a flat-nosed bullet shape variety, but not as long as the later, similarly-shaped indicator lenses. These clear plastic lenses were retained by a very thin metal housing, with the retaining screws running at right angles through the housing and lens. Thankfully for restorers of these early models, these lenses and retainers were also used on Beetles and Type 2s of the same era. The tail lights were located lower down on the rear fender than on the 1960 to 1969 models. The pre-'58 tail lights had a glass segment and were removable from the chrome retainer.

1957 MODEL YEAR

There were few modifications of note in the second model year. Items common to '56 through to '59 models include a rubber matt segment on the floor surrounding the driver's controls, and not full carpeting as in the later, second-generation 'wide nostril' models. Early (pre-'58) models

Left

In 1960 the biggest styling changes in the Type 1 Karmann Ghia's 19-year history were made. The headlights were raised, the front wheel arches were given a greater cutaway towards the rear, the nostril grilles were enlarged and the tail lights were restyled, amongst other changes

featured pressed metal number plate light housings, while later models ('58 onwards) would use a cast metal housing and slightly different light lenses. Notes on these pre-1958 models include the use of pewter for the bumper overriders, and of a translucent plastic for the sunvisors. For the '58 model year different plastic would be used until the 1960 model year.

1958 MODEL YEAR

The year of the cabriolet, and the year of some major changes to the interior. A Karmann Ghia-specific steering wheel was the most noteworthy change, the one you notice first on a '58. This features a half-moon horn/hooter ring and a most attractive grey plastic centre, with a Wolfsburg crest. It was fitted to '58 and '59 Ghia models only, and if you buy a Ghia made during this period, make sure it has this wheel, as Beetle ones are of a completely different style. The centre piece was also

Above
The major distinguishing feature of pre-August '59 (1960 model-year) Ghia is the narrow fresh air vent with two trim slats

Left
This 1959 Coupé still features the original styling, with "droop snout" headlights, and narrower cutaway on front wheelarches. The rear windows were also fixed, whereas 1960 and later models had hinged rear windows for a narrow opening

made of steel for some markets. The other big interior change was the fitting of a fuel gauge. This is of the electrical type, not the later cable-driven one used a few years later. The upholstery was changed, with more ornate door panelling, while the driver's door still retained the pull-strap, in place of an armrest, as on earlier models. The fresh air vent controls were grouped together on the driver's side, while a lockable hood (bonnet) release was fitted to the cabriolet models. The sunvisors were changed to an opaque-patterned, fawn-coloured plastic, still locating via a chromed rod in the mirror mounting.

Convertible models were fitted with a chromed lockable hood release, and a self-cancelling indicator switch was fitted. Those sinuous overrider tubes, curving around the corners on the rear, were fitted to export Karmann Ghias. These used new, larger steel overriders, with a hole to accept the tube. Non-export models (European) had smaller overriders. One piece tail light lenses were fitted, still of the small rectangular shape. The front indicator (park light) lenses were changed half-way through the '58 model year. Of clear glass rather than amber plastic (although up to this point clear plastic lenses were used in some markets), they were more pointed than before and smaller, and retained by a heavier metal chrome ring that fitted over the rim of the lens from the front. The rear brake backing plates were rotated through 180°.

1959 MODEL YEAR
A slight re-design of the hooter or horn button saw the ornate centre section made from steel, with a screw-on mounting. The '58 ones were made of plastic. The window winder mechanisms were redesigned, and the front windows were slightly altered. The rear windows remained fixed, as they had been through from August 1955. The door hinges were redesigned, using alloy with nylon bushings, instead of the previous steel. The dashtop continued to be un-covered metal, painted in body-colour, with a plastic cover for the radio speaker. Seats were covered in vinyl with optional fabric inserts and ornate piping.

1960 MODEL YEAR
The year of the big redesign. The mudguards, or fenders, were re-shaped at both ends, at the rear just slightly to accept the new leaf-shaped tail lights. These were all-red for American markets or red and amber for European-destined Ghias. The front fenders were given raised headlamps and the wheel-arch cutaway was widened, sweeping more towards the rear. Thus the alloy beading strips for the front fenders on post '59 cars are shorter than for the '56 to '59 cars.

The fresh air 'nostrils' were much wider and featured three-slat alloy grilles with an integrated tear-drop-shaped surround. A new, deeply

Above right
The wider nostril, three-bar slats and a plated grille surround, was used from 1960 to 1974, when Karmann Ghia production ceased

Below right
The stubby oblong-shaped taillights fitted to the pre-1960 models. These lenses came in two variations, the earlier ones using glass as well as plastic, and were seperate from the plated frames. The plastic lenses are integrated with the frames

dished steering wheel, now common to Beetles, was introduced with a circular horn (hooter) button and half-round ring.

The rear windows were hinged for the first time and retained with chrome-plated catches, allowing just a small degree of opening. The dashboard was covered for the first time with a vinyl pad and an armrest was fitted to the driver's door in place of the strap.

A windscreen washer (previously optional) was fitted as standard equipment. A new indicator switch, incorporating a headlamp flasher/dimmer, was installed. The doors and front windows featured a slight re-design, making it difficult to fit post-1960 door-glass to earlier models and vice-versa. Mechanically, changes were limited to the fitting of a steering damper to the front suspension.

1961 MODEL YEAR

Just one year after the big change, there was no sense in introducing stylistic up-dates. However, developments in the Beetle department at Volkswagen AG had finally produced the definitive 1200 motor. This year saw the introduction of the 34 hp (DIN) 1200 powerplant, also known as the 40-horsepower motor in countries where the SAE standard of power measurement applied.

This motor is distinguished immediately from its 30-horse predecessor by the seperated, bolt-on generator pedestal. All earlier motors had the pedestal cast integrally with the rest of the right-hand-side engine casing. In later years this motor would be known as the '1200' while the earlier motors would be known among most VW enthusiasts as the 1100. But this is not factually correct as, from 1954 onwards all VW flat-fours were already of 1192 cc displacement, and this displacement was adhered to for the new 1200.

However, internal changes to the new-for-'61 motor were radical. Cylinder bore-centre spacings were increased by 10 mm, the crankshaft received heavier main and big-end bearing journals, the camshaft gave a higher lift, cam followers were re-designed, and the head featured larger valves and a compression ratio raised from 6.6:1 to 7.0:1. A new carburettor, the Solex 28 PICT, with 'hot wire' choke mechanism electrically linked to the coil, and an integral accelerator pump, was adopted.

To go with the new engine an all-new gearbox, with one-piece casing was manufactured. Earlier gearboxes are distinguished by their vertically split casings and these 'boxes had synchromesh only on the upper three gears. The new box had synchromesh on first gear as well, and final drive was made taller from 4.43:1 to 4.375:1. Internal gear ratios were juggled accordingly. These early 1200 34-horse (DIN) motors are also distinguished by the lack of fresh-air ductings in the fan shroud. A new air

Above right
These were undoubtedly the most attractive tail lights fitted to Karmann Ghias, from 1960 through to 1969

Below right
Bigger and, well, not necessarily better. The '70 and '71 models had tail lights very similar to early Type 3 models. From '72 onwards they became even larger!

filter with a duck-bill air intake, replaced the all-round filter fitted until this point. A new fuel tank, which had a flatter top and a tall filler neck was fitted. This tank still used the electrical fuel gauge.

1962 MODEL YEAR

The beautiful nose badges that have distinguished Karmann Ghias from other VW model lines were re-designed for this year and the '62-onwards emblems would continue in production until the 1974 shut-down. Whereas the badges up until this point were one-piece, chrome-plated items with anodising in the relief areas, the new badges were two piece, with the 'VW' logo separate from the circular casting. Interestingly, German-market Ghias built before 1962 featured a dark blue background to the VW logo on the home-market one-piece badges.

The gear-lever was also changed for 1962. Models built up to this period had a thicker, 10 mm lever, while from '62 onwards the lever tapered down to 7 mm at the top, and thus the gear-knobs aren't interchangeable. Knobs were available in black, ivory or grey. The fuel gauge also changed using a cable drive rather than an electrical sending system. This cable-drive system with the different sender unit would be used until the end of the '66 model year in all Type 1 Ghias.

The dashboard grab-handle also underwent a change this year. For '62

Above
Nose badges are another Karmann-specific item and are not interchangeable with Beetle brightwear. This one-piece beauty is common to pre-1962 models

Above right
Nose badges used from 1962-onwards are two piece, with the "VW" logo cast separately from the alloy surround

Right
Very rare in early Ghia production was this one-piece badge with a blue-porcelain centre, used on German models prior to 1962

(continuing up until '67) the grab-handles were made of rigid plastic with moulded grooves, whereas previously they had been aluminium. Both types are removable.

1963 MODEL YEAR

Perhaps the most exquisite piece of design on the Ghia is the famous 'Karmann Ghia' engine lid (or rear deck) metal script. For 1963, the year of the introduction of the razor-edged Type III Ghia, the script shrunk from 30 mm to 23 mm in length. The reason was that Volkswagen could then use a common script for both types of Ghia models.

Another addition in this department was the 'Volkswagen' metal script that appeared on the left side of the vertical plane of the engine cover, alongside the rear licence plate. Inside there was a slight change this year to the kick plate beneath the rear seat. There was also a new door latching mechanism, less robust than the previous system. And changes to the window-winding regulators.

Mechanical changes included the famous fresh air ducting from the fan shroud to the collectors over the exhaust system for the interior heating system. This gave a major boost to the in-car heating system.

1964 MODEL YEAR

Distinguishing a 1964 model from a '63 requires close examination of the front end of the car. The most noticeable change was the switch to the third type of 'bullet-shaped' indicator (or turn signal) lights devised since the car's inception. These look very much like the first type (i.e plated light-metal holder without the separate chrome metal surround, used from late 1958 to early '64) but the lenses are all amber from this point on and the screws locate through the lens itself, in a direction parallel to the car, rather than at right angles as on the first type of lens and holder set-up. The lenses are also larger and arguably the most beautiful of all Ghia indicator variants, as they really flow with the body.

The headlight retainers were also changed. The buckets welded to the body received a lip that enabled counter-lipped new-style, plated retainer rings to grip the bucket rim and be retained by just a single screw at the bottom of the ring. Early rings are very difficult to source now, and expensive if you can get them. Trivia freaks will like the change made to the chrome fittings on the rear elliptical windows. The circular little domes are missing the two indentations that enabled the fitment of a tightening tool on the models produced up until this date.

Inside, the dashboard pad was changed to completely cover the dash-mounted radio speaker. Earlier models (including pre-dash pad models of 1959 and earlier) were all fitted with a plastic speaker grille cover. The '64-and-beyond dash pads have delicate little holes inserted in them to

Above right
The late 1958 to late 1964 Ghias used this front indicator light format, which featured a chromed retaining ring with retaining screws inserted from the front of the housing

Below right
From late 1964 to the end of 1969, Type I Ghias were fitted with this amber, "truncated bullet" indicator lens with a simpler, plated housing

let the sound waves through. Another slight change was made to the steering wheel. The hooter (or horn) activator on the steering wheel was changed to a chromed bar. This would soon revert back to a half moon arrangement in ensuing years.

The inside door handles, up to this point being the ice pick-shaped items used on early Beetles, were changed to recessed levers with a plated metal surround. These (thank the Lord) are Beetle-compatible items, a small concession on Karmann's part to restorers of the future.

1965 MODEL YEAR

Changes on this model were limited mostly to the interior. The easiest model-spotting trick here is a glance at the heater control system. This was the year of the move to twin levers mounted alongside the handbrake lever, getting away from the old-fashioned knob mounted forward on the centre tunnel. These levers came with a red and a white knob and were semi-shrouded by the rubber handbrake boot.

The sunvisors changed in shape, being more oblong, and they were now located close to the 'A' pillars on the roof, to swivel outwards for afternoon sunlight. They were located in the centre via little plastic tabs on the visors and plastic sockets mounted to the interior light. The rear-view mirror and interior light mounting was now integral.

Above
Modernising the Ghia after so many years in production meant concessions to voguish styling trends. Hence these oblong indicator lenses, introduced from 1970 onwards

Above right
From 1955 to 1965 Ghias used the standard Beetle rims and hubcaps, with an exquisite aluminium "beauty" trim

Right
These criss-cross trim rings became extremely popular in the 1960s, being fitted to Beetles as well as Ghias as a dealer optional extra

From this year onwards VW adopted a new chassis numbering system for the Karmann Ghia. Whereas previously the numbering system was integral with Beetle production and consecutive, from the '65 model year onwards the numbers started with the type number. As Karmann Ghias were known as Type 14s within the Volkswagen organization, the numbers all started with 14, followed by one number to designate the year (i.e '5' for 1965 followed by a production number). Thus the numbers ran as follows: 145 000001 to 145 999000 for this model year.

1966 MODEL YEAR

Major mechanical changes were scripted for Ghia production this year. The most notable was to the engine, which increased in capacity from 1192 cc to 1285 cc and horsepower to 40 (DIN) or 50 in SAE measurement. Outwardly, the new '1300' motor looked almost identical to the 1200, but the heads featured a greater number of fins and the carburettor went up in size from 28 mm to a new 30 PICT model Solex.

A new air cleaner arrangement was fitted, using a rubber and metal tube between the carb and off-set. Incidentally all Ghias use Karmann-specific air cleaners, and Beetle ones are not interchangeable. The '66 cleaner bowl was also enlarged, while some '66 models, intended for exported to dusty environments, were fitted with a unique twin-bowl air cleaner. Single-bowl air cleaners were now mounted on the right-hand-side of the engine bay (previously left). The battery was mounted on the left side of the engine compartment, whereas previously it was right-hand-side-mounted. A new ratio for third gear was installed to handle the extra power.

A look underneath the front end confirmed that changes for '66 were radical. Gone was the famous king-pin-link-pin suspension, to be replaced by a ball-joint arrangement, although still attached to the famous twin-beam front end. New wheels were also specified for 1966. The wheels had attractive slots, almost indistinguishable from Porsche 356 rims, still used the five-stud pattern and with drum brakes front and rear. Incidentally these drums are only to be found on '66 models, and thus they are extremely difficult to source in some parts of the world, as they are not generally 'Beetle-compatible'.

New flat hubcaps were used, along with attractive plated "beauty rings" or trim rings with short, wide slots. Inside, there were some notable changes to the interior. Plated, 'metal-look' plastic trim was affixed to the dashboard, running right across from cubby-hole to the far side of the instruments. Also, rather as an afterthought, but nevertheless quite pretty, an ashtray was tacked on beneath the dash, replacing the pop-out one that had survived until this point from the original design. A door-mounted wing mirror was introduced to replace the more beautiful

Right
From 1966 flat hubcaps were introduced, along with slotted wheel rims, but still of the five-stud pattern. The flat-caps were retained by tabs formed into the wheel rim, rather than the riveted spring steel tabs fitted to earlier rims. The trims were an optional factory extra

Below right
Slots on the '66 model wheels are visible here. These wheels are rare as they were only fitted for one model year. A Ghia with these wheels has ball-joint front suspension, but drum brakes

mudguard-mounted item that was fitted to some earlier models.

    This mirror would only be used for two years, before being replaced by a larger mirror of similar design in 1968. Moving outside again, the '66 models are also distinguished by the '1300' script fitted on the vertical plane of the decklid (engine cover) to the left of the number plate (licence holder).

In 1967, four-stud wheels and disc brakes on the front were fitted. The slots in these wheels are shorter than on the '66 models

1967 MODEL YEAR

A year for big changes in running gear. The Ghia came with a new disc-brake front end and four-bolt wheels, front and rear. With the flat hubcaps in place these are hard to distinguish from the '66 wheels, but remove the caps and the old VW 'cookie cutter' design was replaced by a solid inner, much more rigid than before. Wider rear axles were also fitted, giving increased track at the rear (and minimal tyre-to-mudguard

Silver-painted slotted wheels were fitted in the 1970s, as beauty trim rings became unfashionable

clearance for those who are into fitting wide rims and fat rubber).

Of course the big number for this year was the introduction of the 1500 motor. This one used the increased stroke of the 1300 with larger barrels. A '1500' badge was fitted in place of the '1300' introduced the previous year. However, some markets continued to offer the 1300 version alongside the new 1500. Late-night revellers and the simply myopic were delighted that the whole electrical system was up-graded to 12 volts, giving much better lighting power. The dashboard was also changed completely, with new dials. The large clock gave way to a much smaller item, and the fuel gauge was changed back to an electrical unit after a few years of the cable-operated gizmo.

The ignition switch was also enlarged and some models used a steering lock mechanism. One of the changes definitely for the worse was the fitting of a fake woodgrain finish over the dashboard, similar to the stuff used on kitchen tables. It was prone to cracking, to put it mildly.

A 'Karmann Ghia' script, a beautiful miniature of the one on the decklid, was fitted in the centre of the dash. The door locking mechanism was changed to feature plunger knobs on top of the door sills, and some models came standard with seat belts. Interior trim changes included the demise of the triangular-section aluminium mouldings used on the upper door/window sills and the frames below the rear quarter windows. The window winders were changed for chrome, Beetle-like items with black plastic knobs, and so the concave-chamfered knobs fitted specifically to Ghias from 1955 became a thing of the past. The seat squabs or bases were re-shaped after Ghias had used the same basic design (but not upholstery trim) for over a decade. The '67 squabs were recessed to provide more lateral support as more and more people discovered that this little car could actually generate a high degree of lateral Gs with the right driver.

On convertible models a new securing mechanism for the top was devised for the rear, fixed part of the folding hood. Cars up to this point had the top tacked to a piece of wood, but from '67 until the end of production the top was secured by a cable to the rear of the cockpit. This must have been the year for cables and mechanism design fixation. The seat backs were now released via a knob on the backrest, whereas up to this point they tilted forward freely.

1968 MODEL YEAR
This was the year when the Safety shock troops started messing with the design, albeit in a small way. An items of particular concern to Ghia lovers was the appearance of red reflectors on the rear flanks, about half-way between the rear wheelarch and the tail lights.
There were other significant body-panel changes. These included the fitting of a fuel-flap atop the right front wing, which was activated via a cubby-hole (glove-box) mounted lever. Recesses into the doors were pressed to accept new exterior handles. The handles no longer used a protruding knob. The door was opened by slipping your fingers between the recess and the handle and squeezing a lever. Inside safety gear included the first appearance of integral head restraints on the front seat uprights. Owners of '68 models with crumbling seats will be dismayed to learn that these seats were fitted only in '68 and are thus hard to source. A new, black-finished interior mirror was fitted, and the interior light was also restyled. Atop the (still 'wood-covered') dash, a new dash pad, with an integral grab handle for passengers was fitted. At the rear of the cockpit, the famous rubber cord, used for securing the rear seat back, gave way to a plastic clip. A semi-automatic version of the Ghia was also offered this year, using a three-speed 'box and a hydraulic converter in

Above right
About 80 per cent of Ghias doing duty as daily drivers are missing the distinctive side moulding trim. This is made of plated aluminium and consists of 12 different pieces which are not interchangeable. This set is softly rounded, fitted to a 1971 model

Below right
Certain models, mainly pre-1964 cars used a more pointed moulding, of a triangulated shape in cross section. Early cars (pre 1964) also used a metal clip to retain the moulding to the bodywork, and these mouldings have a narrower retaining slot on their undersides. The later mouldings had wider slots to accept a plastic retaining clip

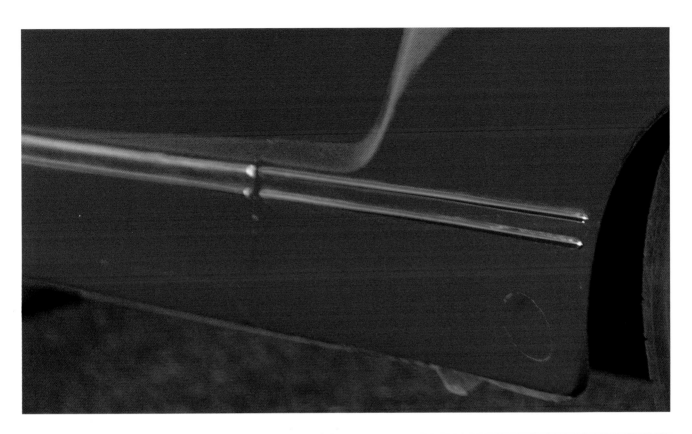

Pre-1960 models had no driver's side armrests fitted. The door was tugged closed by using a leather strap

place of the clutch. This was discontinued after 1969 due to lack of demand. The 1300 versions, which were built alongside the 1500s in '67 and '68, went out of production at the end of this year. The semi-auto versions also featured a new independent suspension system at the rear, which was introduced on all Type 1 Ghias for the following year. A final change was the relocation of the ignition switch to the steering column.

1969 MODEL YEAR

This year will probably be more famous for the Woodstock music festival than for the fact that the 1500 versions alone were offered in '69, or that the highly acclaimed new 'IRS' rear suspension was introduced. This consisted of double-jointed drive shafts with trailing arms, along with transverse torsion bars. Up-rated shocks of the double-acting design were fitted, and this eliminated the famous 'wheel tuck' known to Ghia

Passenger side doors on pre-'60 models had armrests, two-tone vinyl upholstery and three aluminium trim strips similar to the exterior side mouldings

drivers of '68 and earlier models who were fond of exploring the oversteering limits of the car. The seat department at Karmann were kept busy as they produced yet another new seatback, this time with 'pop-up' head restraints mounted on stalks. Changes to the bodyshell included moving the heater outlets to a point next to the seats, instead of towards the front of the footwell.

Convertible models received a completely re-vamped top for this year. Firstly there was the glass rear screen for this year, which made folding the hood a little easier as there was now no chance of putting a crease into the rear screen as there was with the plastic items. The latching mechanism at the front, to secure the hood to the windscreen top, had stayed the same since 1958. Now a completely new twin-lever latching mechanism, doing away with the cute crank-handle and ragged toothed hooks, was adapted.

1970 MODEL YEAR

Not content with the 1500, VW introduced the new 1600 single-port motor in this model year (August 1969 to July 1970). It displaced 1584 cc, and produced 47 hp (DIN) or 57 hp (SAE). This model is distinguished by larger tail lights very similar to those fitted to the Type 3 saloon. The overrider tubes fitted to American models and optional for other markets, were shortened and did not wrap around the sides of the car at the rear. A rather ugly square-shaped reflector housing, which wrapped around the side of the car, was fitted beneath the tail light. A newly-styled 'Volkswagen' script appeared on the left vertical side of the decklid (engine cover) Up front the classic bullet-shaped indicators gave way to wrap-around oblong-shaped indicator lenses.

1971 MODEL YEAR

Volkswagen seemed to be changing engine sizings and outputs like pairs of socks. This year saw the launch of the twin-port 1600 motor with an output of 50 hp (DIN) or 60 SAE horses. There were slight changes to the vent openings on the dashboard pad, and the door locks were once again integrated into the handle, seeing the disappearance of the plunger knobs on the door window-sills. The 'weaved vinyl' look of the stock seat covers, used in almost unchanged form since the early 1960s, gave way to a plain, pleated vinyl. There was also a slight change to the fresh-air valves located at the corners behind the dashboard, connecting the fresh-air pipe with the warm-air system, to promote demisting. The windshield also received some attention, in the form of a different washer nozzle, and the indicator switch and ignition switches changed in this year.

1972 MODEL YEAR

The Ghia was well and truly 'modernised' this year. Even more massive tail lights were fitted to the rear wings, which were angle-cut to accept these lights so they lay back at an angle. The other big change (and I mean BIG) were the fitting of the ribbed, solid-looking bumpers front and rear. These changed the appearance of the Ghia quite markedly, making the car far more voguish for the times, considering that the basic bumper design used until '71 was conceived in the early 50s. No overriders or "American tubes" were used with this type of bumper. Inside, the dashboard is where it underwent its most radical change, receiving two modern, recessed dials for clock and speedo, and the un-loved woodgrain finish was changed to a black veneer with a pebbly finish. Plastic black caps were also fitted to the tops of the inner door sills and beneath the rear quarter windows. A new frame configuration for the quarter windows was also adopted.

Above right
The steering wheels fitted to late 1958 and 1959 models were Karmann-specific and not common to Beetles as in other years. Thus they are much sought after by restorers of these models. Note the unusual hooter button. Dual tone upholstery was standard for early Ghias, but the parcel tray is a retro-fit accessory

Below right
From 1960 onwards, Karmann Ghias again used Beetle steering wheels, this dished one being touted as a major safety advance at the time. Also from 1960, right-hand-drive models were produced for export markets

The vent controls moved to the dashboard and a new, flat, four-spoke steering wheel completed the 'modernisation kit'. Mechanically, the brake calipers for the front discs were updated for this year.

1973-1974 MODEL YEAR (THE FINAL CURTAIN CALL)

Volkswagen and Karmann were well aware that time was running out for the Ghia by this stage and very few changes were made during the final 18 months of production, even though over 20,000 of the cars were still produced during this period. There were a few changes to the bumper configuration (though not its outward appearance) to bring it in line with American regulations, and the rear seat disappeared: Karmann wanted to avoid the expense of having to fashion complicated mounting points for new seat belt regulations for the American market. Almost as an afterthought, the wiper arms were also changed, and '73 to '74 models came with black instead of the anodised silver arms.

Above
The 1966 models featured anodised metal strips running across the dashboard

Above right
The 1966 models featured plain, basket-weave vinyl upholstery in monotone

Right
The owner of this classic '58 has run the car as a daily driver for over 20 years. Note the opaque plastic sunvisors, located in the rear-view mirror mounting

Above
Post-'66 models featured the "Karmann Ghia" script on the dashboard. This layout is from a '71 Cabriolet 1600

Left
This door-mounted mirror was a factory-fit item from 1966 onwards

Above right
In 1967 the 1493 cc motor, developing 44 horsepower at 4000 rpm, was introduced

Right
1967 also saw the arrival of disc brakes and four-bolt wheels

Select a Ghia

Choosing the right Ghia for you is probably easier than choosing the right marriage partner, kitten from a litter of ten or an insurance broker. Nevertheless, you should arm yourself with as much knowledge as possible about the cars before you start waving your platinum credit card. There is a golden rule when it comes to buying old cars, and that is to go for the one in the best condition that you can afford and don't try and buy a rusted-out heap and kid yourself you'll save money with your own restoration.

There are people who make a living out of restoring cars, but generally they practise their craft on somebody else's sheetmetal, and they charge their clients accordingly. These are the guys that drive wacked-out Passats with a front-end shimmy that they bought for 300 bucks, in between working on a 1932 Deusenberg for some LA biogenetics tycoon. They might, just might, have a project or two of their own gathering dust at the back of the workshop, but remember, they have all the facilities and equipment to tackle panel removal, trim polishing, suspension overhauling or motor-massaging. Rather invest in some poor guy's situation where he has already spent truck-loads of hard cash on a restoration and is now suddenly forced to buy a house, send his daughter to university or one of those other real-life situations that intrude on our hobby.

There are obsessives in the car collector-game who devise entire strategies to get first prize. If you are one of these, you'll keep following that illusive little old lady-driven Ghia that has been eased down to the mall once a week and serviced every few hundred clicks by a Wolfsburg-trained super-wrench. Leave notes on the windscreen. Send her flowers. Send her your Frank Zappa collection…

It all depends what kind of car you want. If you want a Cal-look custom you could buy one that has already been given the de-chrome,

Left
Wish that we could all own pristine examples like this collection belonging to Fanie Vos of Bloemfontein, South Africa. The overrider tubes fitted to the '66 model are known as "American" bumpers, but were in fact available as options in other markets

For sale: Only seven carefree owners,
good eye-appeal, Beetle reliability

bumperless, dropped snout look with seats from a Dodge Viper and
steering wheel billetted from titanium. Or you could buy a ratty standard
one; with your candy-apple paint job already misting your eyes you won't
be too concerned about the fact that the 'Made in Germany' plate is
missing from inside the luggage compartment right-inner panel.

For the classic-look fanatics, the first commandment is to buy the car
that has the most original trim in place. Running gear parts, being almost
entirely Beetle-compatible, are much easier to source for Karmann Ghias
than trim items, and some of those period-styled plated fudnuts can cost
a small fortune if you are lucky enough to find them. But take heart; you
could have fallen in love with a 1948 Tucker...

Rarity value has an appeal for us, otherwise we wouldn't be bothering
about Karmann Ghias in the first place, we'd just go out and buy a Ford.
But when it comes to Ghias you have to ask yourself how valuable the

Check for originality when buying a car. Good points on this '59 are the general condition of the bodywork and the presence of hard-to-find pre-'60 "nostril" grilles. The bumpers would need re-chroming and a set of genuine overriders, which are like hen's teeth to track down

particular Ghia's rarity value is to you. If, for instance, you lash out on a '58 convertible, you will be delighted to discover that there were only 1,325 of them imported to the U.S. that model year, or a total of 4,392 made in the '58 calendar year. You may also be driven to the brink of insanity trying to source the steering-wheel for this car, which was only produced in part of '58 and '59 for Karmann Ghias specifically. Not Beetle compatible.

Buying a later model Ghia, you would think, would be a much safer bet, but there are also pitfalls. For instance, the '66 Ghias used a combination of ball-joint front suspension with drum brakes (the discs came the following year with the same suspension). So, finding brake drums for this car is no easy matter, although you can get them, either from dealers with old stock or through specialist firms. With other Ghias, all this type of stuff is readily available from Beetle donor cars.

These are all factors to consider if you intend using your Ghia as a daily driver instead of gazing at it fondly through the dust sheet in your climate-controlled garage. Then there's also the performance bit.

Early Ghias, those produced before '67, have barely adequate power to be used on a day-to-day basis, at least if you want to keep the car standard. Even the 1300 models need to be wound pretty tight to keep up with modern traffic flows in the city, and it's a pain in the butt to keep on moving over to let the hotshots in their Toyotas, Pontiacs or Rovers blast past. But the 1600 models have enough get up and go to perform on a par with most moderns, and in the cruising department, at least on level roads, all Ghias can hang in there at close to 120 km/h (as long as the road stays flat). In fact, the last models were rated for about 135 km/h or close to 85 mph flat-out. Of course, many elderly Ghias have been upgraded with larger motors, and this is a factor to consider if you want to undertake a back-to-original restoration. If the seller says the car is a '63, check out the chassis and engine number parameters for that year, to see whether the motor is original, or if it at least is of the same configuration as the mill used for that particular year.

The same obviously applies to trim items such as handbrake levers, seats, dashknobs, etcetera. Personally I've found that buying an almost complete Ghia (in respect of trim) is perhaps even more frustrating than buying one that has been re-vamped completely, as the items that are missing bug you more than they really should. There is also the tricky subject of taste to tackle. There is no accounting for it, but I may as well go on record that I prefer the earlier Ghias to the later ones, but I can't make up my mind whether the pre-1960, narrow-nostril type is better than the '60-65 type.

I mention these years because they still used the original rounded dome-shaped hubcap, which to my mind synched perfectly with the rest of the Ghia styling. The flat caps looked smarter, perhaps, and less Beetle-like to some, but there was a classic element missing after this. Hmmm. The narrow nostril low-headlight version, the original produced between September '55 and August '59 again has a look that is even more classic than the post '60 models. It has rounder lines, created by the lower lights, the very subtle fresh-air vents with just two tiny little pieces of aluminium acting as grilles, and the tiny tail lights shaped something like a U.S Army sergeant's sleeve patch.

The '50s look is perhaps less graceful than the '60s version, but more

Left
There are cars, and there are cars…When you see a shape like this, you just have to look. It's possible that the driver here has owned the car from new. The light metallic blue paint is particularly attractive on the Ghia

evocative of the great sports car epics of that time, the duels fought out in Ferraris and birdcage Maseratis and Aston Martins, with legends like Peter Collins, Mike Hawthorn and Carroll Shelby grimacing through oil and rubber stains. For perfect balance of form, the relocation of the lights to the top of the fenders completed a design that even today has stylists shaking their heads at the harmony, the purity of it all. The wider nostrils added a more distinctive face to the Ghia without in any way making the car gaudy, and as stated in an earlier chapter, those leaf-shaped tail lights are surpassed for beauty perhaps only by the similarly shaped, but horizontally affixed items found on later model 356 Porsches.

Tastes will also differ as regards the interior. All Karmanns ever built were noted for their superb workmanship and indeed *Road Test* magazine said in its February 1971 report that it was the only car in their experience that rated 100 per cent as far as trim was concerned.

"Perhaps practice does count", they said "but it's still satisfying to sit in a new car and be unable to find a flaw – not only satisfying but extremely rare". If you go for nostalgia, you'll prefer the early interiors, with their hand-stitched look. The dual-tone seats fitted in the '50s and early '60s are marvellous period pieces, as are the pleated map pockets on the door panels and the numerous strips of brightwork lining the door-tops and panels.

The more modern-look cars that evolved seriously in a Beetle compatible direction from 1967 onwards, the year of the woodgrain-like dash, are also popular, and many of the items found in these cars are far more practical for everyday use. Seat belts should be fitted to all cars regardless of year, and head restraints can save your life.

The later pressed, or embossed door panels and seat covers are much easier to source than the earlier items and they look smart without being garish. The final versions of the Ghia were far friendlier from an ergonomic point of view, with knobs, switchgear, levers and steering wheel much more integrated. Dynamically, the '67 and onwards model have a major advantage in the braking department, as those of us with drum brake models will admit after maybe just half a bottle of beer. Not just in outright ability, but in maintenance, as the drums are notorious for wearing out.

Then, of course, there are the convertible versions, the Karmann Ghia cabriolets. There is another rule of thumb touted in the "How-to buy a classic for the least money with the most profit-potential" books,

Originality is hard to come by in 30-year-old cars and some owners choose the modern route of refurbishment. Whatever gets you going…

that a convertible version will be worth 50 per cent more than the equivalent coupé, once the car achieves collector status.

This certainly applies to the Karmann Ghia, which in coupé form was about 50 per cent more, money-wise, than a Beetle when new. It was pretty collectible from day one in coupé form, let alone in ragtop trim. Especially as there was an almost constant waiting list for them at dealers throughout the world during its 19 years of production. Enough sales pitch. The convertible models numbered around 80,000 in total production and although many have been well looked after, many found their way to the scrap heap and many were chopped, changed, messed about and generally allowed to fall into disrepair, if not disrepute.

The most important item when buying a convertible is the top, because the other parts are easier to source. The fabric itself is not the

Above
Of course, the owner's real party trick is the removal of the top, turning his car into a cabriolet – almost. He carried out the remarkably professional conversion himself, to create a hard-top Ghia, an idea that Karmann almost went ahead with way back in the 1950s!

Right
A set of Empi-look-alike wheels and a candy-apple paint job helps this Ghia stand out from the crowd. Probably 80 per cent of Ghias still on the roads have been customised in some way

be-all and end-all, but rather the frame, which consists of dozens of pieces, many of them almost impossible to re-fabricate.

Early models came with a canvas or mohair hood, while later on canvas or vinyl were available, but personally, the mohair hood is worth every extra penny you spend on it. Some people in the carriage trade reckon that there was never a finer convertible top made for any car, with the possible exception of the Mercedes 300 SLs. Wind leakage was at a minimum when they were installed correctly and the trim and mechanism were of the highest order.

What's more, the Karmann convertible still looked extremely handsome with the hood up, something that can't be said for, say, the Porsche Speedster, the Maserati Spyder or any number of cabriolets. Inside, there were no unsightly hinges, frame-tubes or crank mechanisms to be seen. The Ghia Cabriolet came not only with a headliner, but an inner absorbent material, not unlike a carpet underfelt, to give the smoothest of looks when erect. And when the top was down, the cutest of hood-boots was provided to tuck away the paraphernalia so you could soak up the sunshine without worrying about your girlfriend's hair getting caught in one of the pivot points.

Prices for used Ghias fluctuate wildly, but at the time of writing the British magazines, notably *Thoroughbred and Classic Cars*, pitch coupé prices at £1,000 for a really ratty coupé to £7,500 for a pristine example. Cabriolets are listed at £2,500 for a chicken coop to £9,500 for one approaching perfection. These upper prices assume that the car is original in all respects. Generally, a car that has been altered in any way from original loses value, although this doesn't apply to some of the superb Cal-look Karmanns featured in the American mags, *VW Trends*, and *Dune Buggies* and *Hot VWs*.

Left

Expect to pay up to 50 per cent more for a cabriolet version. And this rare '58 is worth plenty! Respected classic car journals peg the value of a cabriolet "in excellent, but not necessarily concours condition" at around £10,000

Tune In

Many people associate air-cooled Volkswagens with rough-and-readiness. Harsh vibes emanating from beyond the rear seat, aural sensations akin to post-hangover gargling, strangled crickets trying to escape down the exhaust pipe, jarring misfires above 4000 revs. But this need not be the case. A well-tuned Vee-Dubs mill, bone-stock or modified, can be the sweetest powerplant on the block. It's just that the things run forever even when in a shocking state of tune, with leaky carbs, cylinder blowby, rusted-out exhausts, shot distributors. It takes more than all this to kill a Bug or Ghia motor, and so many people accept this as their lot in life and drive on and on and on...

An expertly-tuned VW engine should hum rather than rasp and should be virtually vibe-free unless you insist on changing up at 7000 come heat-wave or blizzard. Most engines don't respond well to being over-revved and a VW is more sensitive than most in this regard. Change up well before those speedo lines say you should and you'll be well rewarded. Just as you will if you keep your engine and the rest of your Ghia in good shape. This is not meant to be a workshop manual, as there are far more knowledgable people who have already written more than you would ever want to know about flat-four VW motors. (While on this subject, an indespensible book that springs to mind is the "How to keep your VW Alive" manual for 'compleat idiots' written by the late, great John Muir; also *VW Beetle Restoration/Preparation/Maintenance* by Jim Tyler.) However, there are a few very basic tricks that you can do yourself that'll save you money, smooth out your day and get you relating to your Ghia on an even deeper level even without buying a hard-to-decipher shop manual.

ENGINE

The first thing to ascertain is whether your engine is in fundamentally good shape. The best way to do this is to have a compression check done, not the easiest thing in the world given the confines of the Karmann engine compartment, but at least it's better than practising surgery in the Beetle's glove-box-sized bay.

A compression reading on a healthy motor should be in the region of

The famous Solex carbs fitted to Volkswagen motors during the Karmann Ghia's life-span ranged in size from 28 mm, through 30 mm to 34 mm. They are easy to keep in fine fettle

Low-cost Brazilian-made silencers like this are available at bargain-basement prices. The complex system, which incorporates the air-cooling system as well as in-car heating, can be a real headache to replace

700 to 1000 kPa for all cylinders, and if there is a big discrepancy between any of them, there could be a number of reasons, some less pleasant than others to contemplate. Given a lousy reading, check that you don't have a valve that is sticking open owing to tightening up of the rocker gear. Clearances for the valves should be in the region of .004 of an inch (four thou) for motors built up to 1960, .008 intake and for inlet and exhaust for all the others. This is a good first tune-up step to tackle, even if it does mean jacking the car up and squirming underneath like you used to do so easily when you were young and carefree.

ALWAYS insert axle stands before crawling underneath the car. Hydraulic jacks have been known to fail, sometimes without any warning and you'd hate to be known as 'ol' fin-face'. To adjust the valves you'll have to remove the tappet covers, an easy-enough chore as they are held together by stout metal clips. Be prepared for some oil to drip down, so allow this to happen before you stick your face underneath to have a looksee. Wipe away excess oil, and in fact, preferably drain the engine oil before even attempting this job, as it'll be a good idea to change the oil now that you've gone to so much trouble.

Loose tappets, or rocker clearances, will mean that your car isn't enjoying the amount of valve lift it should, and thus you can expect an increase in performance when you've set them correctly. You can do this by cranking over the engine just a touch with the starter key, or get someone to turn the motor over manually, via a large spanner on the crank-pulley nut. It makes life a lot easier if you remove the spark plugs before you do this, and come to think of it, this is also a good time to replace those old plugs anyway, once you've finished setting the valve clearances. Remember to crank over the engine a few times to re-check the clearances, just in case you set one of the valves before the camshaft lobe had peaked.

A lack of valve clearance on one of the valves could be good news, in that you may have found your reason for a lack of compression, and cured it just by adjusting the valves. Valves can tighten up with wear as they 'pocket' themselves more deeply into the head, causing the stem to stick out further and thus run into a non-clearance problem with the rocker tip. However, the tight valve could also be due to a problem with the valve seat which is preventing the valve from seating at all, in which case you'll have to pull the motor out and remove the head to effect a cure. And when you've gone this far, you may as well go deeper, whip off the other head to check the ridge on the bores to determine wear and maybe you'd just as well strip the whole thing down at this point, or hand the motor in at an engine exchange shop for a new sub-assembly.

But let's get back to where we were. If the valve clearances are okay but compression is still down, it probably means that the ring landing on one of the pistons has burnt out. This will probably be accompanied by some rich-running characteristics, such as black exhaust smoke which has occurred rather suddenly. But if your car suddenly starts running rich don't immediately suspect the pistons and tear the motor apart. It could be the carburettor at fault. Check that the choke is operating the way it should, which is easy to see on most models: the little ragged tooth tab on the choke spindle, which is activated by a thermostat on the side of the Solex PICT, is exposed to show off its hard work.

If the choke is working okay, it could be that you have a leaky float that is causing fuel levels in the float chamber to rise and richen the mixture. Again this is easy to check, as is a faulty needle and seat, which would trigger similar symptoms. For a stock motor, there is nothing much wrong with the standard vacuum advance Bosch distributor, although many tuners go for the famous Bosch 009 mechanical advance distributor as soon as they buy an air-cooled VW.

The first step is to fit a new set of points. Early models used different contact breakers, so it is a good idea to quote your distributor number when ordering the new set, or better still, take along a sample. You should also buy a new condensor when replacing the points as a matter of course. When replacing the points apply just a touch of grease to the distributor cam lobe which activates the points and adjust the points gap to 0.016 in (sixteen thousandths of an an inch). According to the manufacturers, a strobe-type timing light should be used to set timing, and if you have one of these, good luck. For the rest of us, it is possible

The stock Bosch vacuum-advance distributor needs to be in fine fettle to obtain optimum performance from a Ghia. Many enthusiasts replace it with the famous 009 distributor, also made by Bosch, which offers more accurate spark timing

and perhaps even preferable to set the timing static, with engine switched off. The most accurate way of static setting is to hook up a light bulb (6 or 12 Volt, depending on what system your car runs) to the terminal on the coil that links the points, while the other point on the bulb should be grounded on a metal piece of the car. You turn the engine over to the point where the points should open and for this purpose the manufacturers were thoughtful enough to include timing marks on the crankshaft pulley, in the form of little notches cut out of the wheel on the inner edge of the pulley.

Line up the notch with the point where the engine casing splits. Then hop inside the car, switch the ignition on, but leave the engine off. Grab hold of your bulb device, earth it out properly and if your timing is right, the light should glow. The point at which the light begins to glow is the point where the contact breakers open and the engine fires. This should correspond with the correct timing mark on the pulley and if it doesn't move the distributor, either clockwise or anti-clockwise, until you get a warm glow, on the bulb and deep inside your heart. On the models built between 1955 and 1965 there were two notches on the pulley. The left side one was set at 7.5° BTDC and the other at 10° BTDC. In 1967 there were two nocthes. The one on the left is 7.5° BEFORE TOP DEAD CENTRE (BTDC) and the one on the right is 10° BTDC. Later models had three marks, the one on the lfet being 0° (or TDC), the middle one 7.5° while the right one was 10° BTDC.

To set your timing, the first step is to loosen the distributor pinch bolt so that you can turn the unit by hand, but so that it's not so loose as to swing about easily. On all Ghia models built before 1965 the timing should be set at 10° BTDC. On models built between '66 annd '67 the static tim,ing should be set at 7.5° BTDC. The 1968 to 1970 models were and later were set at TDC (static) but details given out by the factory for models later than this were applicable for timing light (the strobe type) settings, at idle speed. If you own one of these, your best bet would be to mark the distributor where it is currently set in relation to the engine casing and then have the thing set by an approved dealer with all the right workshop manuals, strobe lights and diplomas on his wall. Once you get the car back, simply mark the distributor up at its new setting. If the old and new marks correspond you were running the right timing. (Of course there is the possibility that he didn't set the timing, so maybe you should stand over him and watch while he does the job).

For those of us too lazy for all this, a quick way is to prise off the distributor cap and see at what point the points seem to be opening. They should begin to break contact very close to the marks on the pulley, and if they do, you know you are in the right ball park. As long as

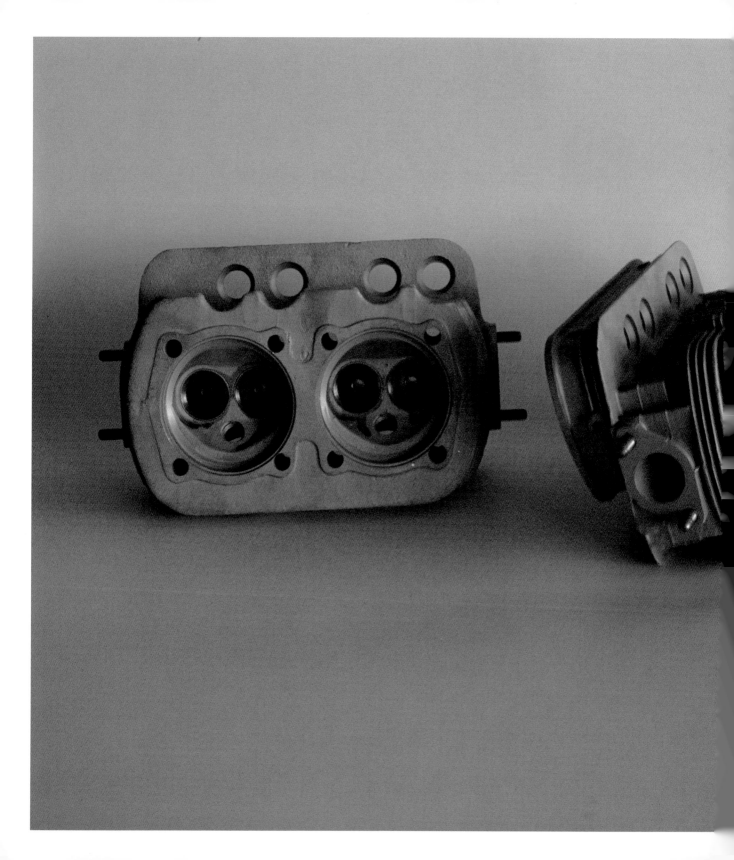

your car doesn't ping (detonate) as you ram your foot flat when the engine is lugging at low revs in a high gear, you know the timing isn't too advanced. Another way of detecting when the timing is too advanced is when the engine is difficult to start. It may spin for a few revolutions and then cause the starter motor to stall. Back off the timing a few degrees and you may well have cured your problem.

As for the rest, a few little tips may come in handy. A roughness when you blip the throttle, and even when out on the road, may be due to a generator in poor condition or out of adjustment. The genny belt tension is adjusted by removing the outer pulley and inserting spacers which increase the taper and the tension of the belt. If the generator bearings are shot, this will also lead to a rough-feeling motor and it will be a good idea to replace these before you destroy the inner windings when the bearings collapse. A high-pitched whining noise will probably give you a few miles' warning of impending disaster. As for the rest of the car, there are various grease points around the suspension that should be attended to if any squeaks develop. And as for the brakes…

Drum brakes on a Ghia can bring lots of unease into the home. The drums tend to wear oval after usage, which gives a sort of ABS effect as the pedal goes hard and soft when you apply the anchors, and this in turn sets up a very individualistic approach to traffic lights, four-way stops and the like. Experts say the drums should only be skimmed once before replacement. A tip for those skimming drums is to supply the machine shop with the wheel and tyre bolted to the drum, so that it can be skimmed round in the form in which it will be used. The drums are notorious for deforming once the wheels are attached to them, leaving them out-of-round. A good tip is to mark your wheel in relation to its position on the drum, so that it always goes back the same way.

Left

It is possible to increase the compression ratio of the Beetle motor by a modest amount with useful gains in performance. If you do skim the heads, remember then to run on premium grade fuel. These are early 30-horse items

The Way of Restoration

This chapter is not a blow-by-blow account of a complete restoration, – that would fill up a couple more books. These books are available, not on Karmann Ghias, but on Beetles and most of the knowledge can be transposed to a Ghia application with little difficulty.

There are also a number of books on restoration in general, detailing what kinds of chisel heads are best used for cleaning out the drain plugs of models built between 1922 and now. Many of these are well worth a read. Your hard-core restorer would give advice diametrically opposed to the counsel given in Chapter five – going for the best-condition Ghia you can. Restorers generally like to find a nose section in Bombay, a tail section in Fiji, then set about fabricating the roof and floorpan, before hand-chiselling the running gear parts just so's it's done right.

If you do go for a burnt-out bombshelter of a car, make sure you pay absolutely next to nothing for it, and that you are able to tackle major panel restoration such as welding, seam-filling, priming and painting yourself. And that you have a sure-fire source for parts tied up, or a retired uncle who is a maestro-machinist with a few decades' time on his hands The most important point when buying a Ghia is to try and get a rust-free one. If that trips all the U.K. Ghia lovers into hysteria, let's amend it slightly to "as free of rust as possible."

Some people reckon that Type I Karmann Ghias are notorious rust traps, but I was able to buy a twenty-something year-old car with virtually not a bubble or a brown stain on it. It all depends on where you live, where the car has lived, but most importantly, how it has been looked after.

If you are scrap-yard hunting in a dry region, don't immediately assume that the car standing out in a field is rust-free just because it hasn't rained in the area for the past seven years. Grass growing up, under and around a car can play havoc with floorpans, sills, engine bays

Left
Anything is restorable, it all depends on how much time and money you want to spend. But to produce something as head-turning as this custom beauty sparkling in the California sunshine requires a level of commitment and expertise few possess

Sill areas in the Ghia are notorious rust traps as are the lower rear wings

and nose sections as it is invariably covered with dew in the early morning. A few weeks of this won't make much impression but after a few years your dewey- eyed dream may be rusted-out completely on the underside. Panel-straightness is probably the most important thing to look for when going for a body that you are planning to rebuild to pristine shape. Look carefully down the sides of the car for ripples or any signs of bodyfiller. Mechanicals are less crucial in a Ghia, as they are in the main Beetle-compatible. Trim, upholstery, seating and all the glass bits are the aspects to worry about and you can read more about these in the next chapter.

When you are talking restoration, you are talking about a car that will look like new once you have finished. If your aim is to merely drive a hot-shot sporty looking car that doesn't cost you much money, you can probably skip most of this chapter. Just look at the pictures and dream. But as someone who has undertaken a half-baked restoration on a completely different make of car, I can tell you that if you go for a quick blow-over spray job, a rough weld or two on the chassis and El Cheapo seat covers, you will never be truly happy with your car. Especially after your first day out with the local Ghia club in your area, as car restorers are, um…commendably up-front when it comes to giving their opinions.

If you are serious about restoration, the best way is to pull the body off the floor pan. That way you'll be able to restore the pan properly and access all those hidden cables, heater controls, suspension members, the gearbox and the brake lines without breaking your back. You can either

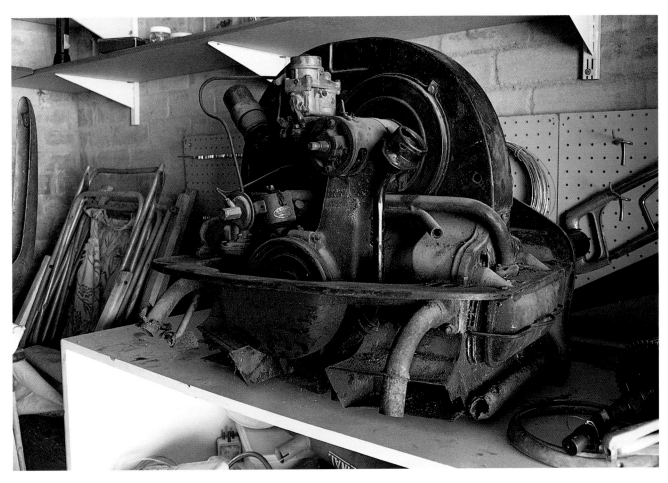

The trend in Ghias these days is towards restoration rather than California-look customising. If you are restoring a pre-1960 model, the motor for you is the "1100" 30-horse old-timer, which is becoming rather rare

pull the engine out before you lift the body or leave it in, once you've disconnected everything relevant. Either way, you are in effect lifting the body over the engine, so you may as well leave it in, although there is going to be more chance of whacking the body against the fan-housing during the crucial body lift, which will require lots of muscle power. The body is bolted to the floor pan via a number of stout bolts and flat tab washers, and these can be removed with no problem.

To make the body itself as light as possible for the lifting process, it is a good idea to remove the front and rear screens and the glass from all four windows. Be careful here, as this glass is extremely rare, and you won't find it at the corner spares shop. Glass for Ghias really should be quoted under the precious commodity heading on the business pages. To get at the door glass you will have to remove the handles and winders which are held in place either by screws or dowel pins, depending on the types of handles fitted. Be extra careful when doing this to avoid tragedy.

The arm rests are mounted to a bracket behind the panel that hooks the panel in place, and once you have the handles removed, lift the panel upwards to get them clear of the door. This was never intended to be a workshop manual so we won't get any further into a step-by-step procedure number here. Arm yourself with a good Beetle repair manual Bentley or Haynes are good, (*and Osprey superb: Ed*) to enable you to deal with the mechanical side of disconnecting wiring that connects the body to the engine. Trace all the wring you can see to its source, and to do this you may have to remove the sound-deadening material on the rear bulkhead, which you will want to replace anyway, although try not to tear it too radically. It will make a nice template for later. The major wiring loom between the front and rear of the body is located in a tube that runs down the side of the body itself, through the door sill. So, unless someone has fitted radio speakers with wiring running along the floor you shouldn't have a problem with wiring snagging body-to-floorpan once you have unplugged the engine-related wiring.

The fuel tank should be drained and removed. The heater tubes should also be disconnected and the steering rod and casing removed as this runs through the bodywork. In fact, remove the carpets and seats at this point too, as they are likely to get hurt during the big heave-ho, which will require about six of your stronger friends (and you sitting on a beer crate directing it all with the promise of exposing the contents of the crate once the job is completed).

Label all the stuff carefully, which is not easy when your hands are dirty, but do it anyway. You may remember where the parts go now, but in a few days things will be getting a bit hazy and in a few years, when you finish your restoration well... A good system is to set up shelves with boxes laid out – the trays that you buy beer or cola cans in are good for this. Designate a box to each section of parts so that you store them in a way that prevents the right rear tail light clip from getting mixed up with the relay for the hooter. Put all the parts in plastic bags for storage, and then set yourself objectives so that you tackle a small task – say, cleaning and polishing the wiper motor – for an evening. By bagging the parts you will prevent them from deteriorating any further, and by keeping them separate and tackling each job in turn you'll concentrate more on that job, do it more thoroughly, learn more about the parts and their function. The body should be mounted on trestles, and take care to support it so that it doesn't damage any of the underpinnings or sag too much in the middle

If you are going to undertake major panel re-fabrication on the body, wait until you have refitted it to the floorpan. The body does tend to flex once you've removed it, and you may weld in a panel that looks nice and

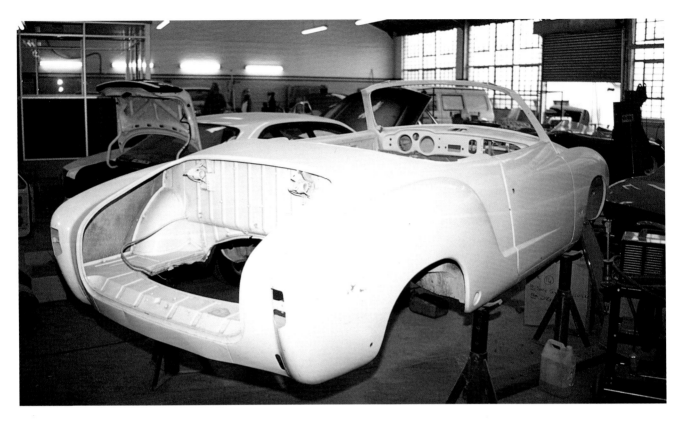

The rarest of all Ghias is the '58 cabriolet, and if you can find a body shell in good condition like this, don't even hesitate: Buy!

straight while it is off the car, but won't line up once you bolt the whole assembly together once again. Scrape out and paper down every little groove in the bodywork, floor pan and on the engine parts and get them spotless before painting them. You'll be amazed at what a difference this makes to a restoration, when you see a perfectly-formed pressing nicely painted, as opposed to something that has been painted over a few times and becomes clogged with paint. Fit new parts, or clean them to perfection if they are still good, even in places where the average person won't see them. This does amazing things for the psyche.

With the body removed, the carpets removed and all the engine oil drained, it is a good time to tip the whole chassis assembly onto its side so you can examine the pan for rust. Don't be deceived by an undersealer job, it may just be covering up rust that is waiting to poke through the moment you get your whole car together again. Ideally, the floorpan should be stripped of all its suspension componentry and sent to a sand or bead blaster for thorough cleaning.

Acid-dipping is another way of removing corroded metal. If you have rusted-out sections, these can be ordered from specialists to be re-welded into your pan, or indeed, it is possible to fit a whole new pan. Remember to get your paper work on the car changed if you change this as the pan carries the original engine number. Also remember that the Ghia pan is different to the Beetle one, in that it is wider and the curve at the front wheel arch area is more dramatic.

The pristine pan should be acid-etch-primed, painted and then coated with undersealer. The more coats of undersealer you apply the better the insulation from road noise, but don't overdo it. Do this on both the floor side and the road side of the pan. Fit generous amounts of underfelt to the pan before fitting new carpets. You may source these from your local upholstery trimmers or order up ready-made ones from specialist firms. Apply this kind of attention to detail to all the parts that you strip, store, clean, replace and refit.

Having parts re-plated is often necessary if the chrome has deteriorated, but examine the output of the plating works before you send them all your cherished unobtaniums. Like painting, the most important part of re-plating is in the surface preparation, so make sure you send the plating works perfectly smooth items. If you can't beat or sand them straight yourself, get a qualified panel beater to do it for you.

Like packed-up layers of old paint, nothing destroys the effect of a restoration so quickly as the retention of cracked rubbers for the screens, doors, lights, badges etc. Order new ones from a reputable firm that deals in either NOS (New Old Stock) items or high quality reproduction fittings. Warning! Some of the rubber offered is almost impossible to use and can lead to a cracked screen or two when trying to refit glass, so it is worthwhile splashing out the greenbacks on good rubber. Again, ask around first.

The engines will be discussed in a bit more detail in a later chapter, but one of the points you could consider at this stage is having all the engine tin-wear powder-coated in black. This gives an easy-to-clean gloss and looks fantastic, as well as retaining the correct original feel. The customisers will go for tangerine fan-housings with brown tappet covers but that's cool, as long as we're all expressing ourselves.

It is also a good idea to have all the bolts and nuts used in the restoration electro-plated. It makes the job look so professional. Some people really like cadmium plating, but I prefer the look of old fashioned galvanizing for that more antique look. It's cheap to do, it makes dealing with your old bolts a lot more pleasant, and those that you have to replace should be ordered with similar plating to match up.

Scrape away all undersealer on the inside of the mudguards, the bulkhead and other out-of-the way places, sand the surface down, etch-primer and apply undersealer while the body is off. By the way, if you are fitting new trim items that previously weren't on the old unrestored car,

The nose sections in the spare-wheel well areas of all Ghias are extremely vulnerable to rust and factory replacement panels are now almost impossible to find. Other parts, such as fenders, sills and doors are still obtainable, however

such as beadings, headlight rims etc, it is a good idea to trial-fit all this new stuff in place first before having your bodyshell painted. This way you'll make all your mistakes before being confronted by a virgin paintjob that you won't want to scratch. You'll end up doing a lot of the restoration twice, but results are what we are after here. Ask lots of questions when you meet a Ghia owner as to the correct bits for your car, and don't take the first guy's word for it. I've met dozens of Ghia owners and their knowledge ranges from nonexistent to encyclopaedic, but you may be unlucky enough to meet an encylopaedia salesman who wishes he was a Ghia expert. Get a second, third and fourth opinion before lashing out on a new set of door panels or indicator lenses. Time is of no essence when it comes to a restoration, although it is a good idea to set yourself realistic goals as you go along.

The state of mind you should achieve is one similar to that recommended by Alcoholics Anonymous, of taking one day at a time. And come to think of it, restoring a car is a pretty good substitute for spending your time in a bar, if that happens to be one of your lifestyle signifiers that you'd like to modify.

Body Language

There is something besides rust that chews up body panels and spits them out more unsightly than a stream of chewing tobacco. That little something is known as driver error, when you just clip a curb and next thing that beautiful five-piece Ghia nose has turned into a falafal and the headlights are scrabbling for traction on the tarmac. It may not be you at fault. Enter the harassed commuter in his Metro/Cutlass/Golf who turns around to admonish the truck driver nosing out of the side street, and shunts your pride and joy up the rear. Eeeshhh.

The thought of this happening is almost enough to make you want to sell your Ghia and drive something like a Fiat Panda, where parts are being churned out faster than they can be written off. That's the thing when disaster strikes a Ghia – getting hold of those elusive body parts.

The good news is that the panels originally specified by Karmann were extremely stout, and a good bodyshop man should probably be able to repair most damage. But ideally panels should be replaced in the event of a shunt, or severe corrosion, which is likely to occur in a number of places around the car. The most likely place for corrosion to take place is in the nose, beneath the spare wheel, where the hooter resides. Also in this area, the valance beneath the well traps a fair bit of wet stuff.

The other big rust trap is set in the sills, which is not that extraordinary an occurrence in just about any kind of car made from steel. The wheel arch liners also tend to corrode, while another high risk spot is the area behind the rear wheel arches. The doors themselves are prone to bubbles on their lower edges, while later models have been known to rust out on the upper window sills, because of different rimming fitted in the last few years of production acting as a rust trap.

The seals for wind screen and rear screen are very well designed and it is unusual to find a Ghia rusting in these areas, unlike many modern

Right
Detailing is what makes the difference between a good restoration and a so-so car. Note the overrider tube bumpers on this car, which are becoming difficult to find, as are all bumper parts

hatchbacks. The engine lid is prone to the brown bug at its lower leading edge. That's the bad news. The good news is that replacement wings, sills noses and the like are still to be found for Ghia, through various sources. One of these is the world-wide Volkswagen dealer network itself, although NOS (New Old Stock) items are becoming exceedingly scarce as supplies run out, and many will have to turn to reproduction or second-hand replacement bits. In this line of work there are a number of enterprising establishments situated in the United States and in the U.K and there are some in Australia and New Zealand. There was even one

Above
Going the custom route means greater freedom of choice in terms of trim parts. This topless conversion uses many modern items sourced from other cars, but still looks very good indeed

Right
If you have the space, buying a complete shell for good rebuildable body parts is a good idea

Overleaf
There are many aftermarket suppliers of cabriolet tops in the U.S. If you are buying a wrecked cabriolet, the most important item on your parts checklist is the frame. For the fabric, you have a choice of vinyl, which is cheaper, canvas or mohair. Mohair tops look far more authentic

in South Africa, although most of the trim bits in the author's homeland have since been snapped up by restorers and as this was written only second-hand body parts were available. See the 'Contacts' list at the back of this book for more information.

The Ghia restoration people are a fantastic source of information on Ghias, and in fact many of these firms produce catalogues that are the closest thing you'll get to a workshop manual on the cars. Not that they tell you how to refurbish a valve guide or anything like that, but they provide exploded-view drawings of many of the parts, which will enable you to set about dismantling, or more important, piecing together, your new-found obsession.

Many of them offer both new, used and reproduction parts, and such is the interest in Ghias that they are continually producing new reproduction parts to cater for the thousands of Ghias still on the roads. Indeed, Scott Dempster of Karmann Ghia Parts and Restoration in Santa

Above
From 1968 onwards, the doors featured a recess for the outside door handle, which was of a completely different design

Left
Note when buying doors that they are not all interchangeable. Changes to the 1960 doors means that window glass is not interchangeable with earlier models

Barbara, Ca., estimates that 20% of Ghias exported to the United States are still on the road, which would put the figure close to 70,000. The little beauties are rarer in the U.K., in South Africa they are rarer still, and funnily enough even in Germany, the host country, they aren't exactly thick on the ground. Nevertheless, Volkswagen produced body parts for Karmann Ghias until 1988, and so, scattered around in various dealerships around the world you still may find a genuine VW-stamped brand new nose section, wing, bonnet (hood) or engine lid. There is nothing wrong in using second-hand replacement panels as long as they are devoid of rust and properly prepared for painting.

Just in case you rushed through the 'Differences' chapter, there are a few items to note when scrap-yard scouting. The difference in light height between pre-1960 front wings and later ones will make your car look like it's frowning on one side and startled on the other. Also the

These pressed-steel rims were known as "Rostyle" wheels in some countries. They were fitted as standard to special edition Beetles in the 1970s, but never on Ghias

Variation on the smooth Cal-look Ghia. Note the lack of trim and the absence of fresh-air "nostrils". Fibreglass bumpers are available from U.S. aftermarket concerns, much cheaper than originals!

nostril grilles are quite different. The same goes for the rear wings. The '59 and earlier models took the smaller back lights, although to convert to later lights on the rear wings would not be such a problem. Refer to Chapter Five on other various changes to body panels over the years.

The doors on the '59 models, for instance, underwent a change that prevents you from using glass from these and later models on earlier cars. A good body man could effect a cut and weld job to enable you to do so if you were desperate, and when it comes to glass most people are. Glass is still available from the odd accredited Volkswagen dealer, so always check first before travelling 1,000 miles to a scrapyard. But, if you are lucky enough to source NOS glass, be advised that it won't come cheap. Later doors, as mentioned in Chapter Five, featured a recess to enable you grab the differently-styled door handle. This change happened in 1968. Having to fill in the fuel flap on fenders of '69 and later models

so that you can use them on earlier models is not a major problem, and nor is adapting the indicator lights from pre 1970 "wrap-around" models to earlier ones. It just makes life a lot easier to know which one to go for if you are confronted with a choice of various panels, and a spares salesman who's new at the Ghia game.

Headlights look very similar on models but they aren't. The early, low-lighted models (pre '59) had slightly smaller lenses and different mounting systems. In addition, the headlight buckets welded into the body have a different lip which prevents you from using the later design.

Early headlight arrangements are still available, and in fact Hella dealers still stock many of the headlights and tail lights for Ghias, but they are pricey. Second-hand lights are to be found for the pre-'60 cars, but if you can't unearth any, another option is to find some scrap post-'60 headlights, mounting mechanisms and buckets, and have the buckets welded in. Many Beetle parts will fit on Ghias but are not of the same original design. This goes for steering wheels of certain models, and the knobs found on the window winders and dashboards of earlier models. The early model Ghias used knobs of an extremely elegant concave-curved design that are very similar to the Beetle's straight-line taper, so look out for this. The same goes for the handbrake lever. The Beetle handbrake will fit and function on a Ghia but it is shorter and less in keeping with the sleek looks of the car.

Upholstery panels are Ghia specific and you can buy good reproductions of the later types with moulded grooves. But for earlier types it would be best to get an upholstery trimmer to copy patterns out of similar material for that authentic look. Body parts aren't cheap for Ghias, but then they shouldn't be on a custom coach-built coupé or convertible, which has maintained its good looks long after racier, more flighty types have fallen off the road.

Left
The ideal car for the coast. This "smoothy" is owned by a Durban artist. The Rickshaw driver in the background wants a ride!

Engine Massaging

There are countless firms, mainly Stateside, offering go-faster items for Volskwagen air-cooled motors. All very well and good, but before you bolt a pair of Weber 48 IDAs to your Ghia, you should really do a full rebuild on the motor. This means making sure that the engine casings have been properly mated . Have them machined if they are at all suspect, as you don't needed leaky casings in your life, you can buy some tin-plate from Detroit for that pleasure.

After long usage the crank starts rattling around in the casings. Worn casings should be line-bored, which means machining the crankshaft main bearing surfaces at an angle absolutely perpendicular to the cylinder head facings. Among other items of interest which you should ask your potential reconditioned engine salesman about is whether the valve seats have been replaced, as these are notoriously wayward on some twin-port 1600 motors.

The flywheel surface where the clutch makes contact should be surface ground to exacting specifications, and there are all sorts of other little tricks with VW motors that an expert knows by heart, but a VW novice, even one who has built countless water-cooled motors, wouldn't be able to tell you. One of these is setting up the correct end-float in the crankshaft by means of washers between the crank and the flywheel. Again, this is a task that is vital to a long-running motor. Also make sure that the oil cooler has been thoroughly cleaned, that the oil pump produces the rather high pressure for what is essentially an oil- as well as air-cooled motor, and that certain vital pieces of tin-plate have been replaced which direct air to the right places.

Right
The "1100" motor, which is in fact an 1192 cc displacement, but is confused with the pre-1954 Beetle motor, which was a 1131 cc mill. Better to describe it as a 30-horse (DIN) motor, identified by the solid casting of the upper casing that included the generator pedestal. Later 1200s (Post 1960) produced 34 horsepower (DIN) and these motors had the generator pedestal bolted to the engine casing

Above right
The common or garden variety, the definitive VW 1200 motor, as fitted from 1961. Note the Karmann-specific off-set aircleaner, the separate generator pedestal and the overall immaculate condition! This is the 34 horse (DIN) motor, often known as the 40 horse (SAE) motor. Concentrate…

Below right
The 1285 cc motor, fitted from 1966. Note the updated aircleaner arrangement, which helped this motor produce 40 bhp (DIN)

This book is meant as a celebration of a great automotive design and for some, a companion to Ghia ownership, not a manual that you keep alongside your grease-gun (otherwise we wouldn't have gone to the trouble and enormous expense of reproducing all those pretty pictures all over the place). For detailed engine refurbishing you should buy one of the many good workshop manuals available. The same goes for tuning advice. There are numerous books on this, and seeing as Okrasa , Empi, Gene Berg *et al* have become almost as legendary as the Ghia and Beetle, we'd have to conclude that there is a strong case to be made for squeezing more than 50 horses out of a 1930s design. I'm not sure what the ultimate power figure for a VeeDubs flat-four is at the moment among the Johnny's Speed and Chrome brigade, but it probably runs at around 200 for a normally aspirated motor, albeit one that isn't really streetable. Big bore kits are available in a range of sizes normally up to 94 mm, while stroked cranks, some of them of forged steel, are available up to 92 mm, some of them offering full circle counterweight webbing for ultra-high-revving motors. With these you can bump your engine's capacity up to 1.7-litres, 1.8 or even over the two-litre threshold.

Cams range from mildly uprated to wild, and carbs likewise. You can tack a twinchoke 36 DCD Weber onto your stock manifold, with a few modifications, go for the streetable Kadron dual 40 mm down draught kit, or if you are really serious, go to IDA type Webers, right up to 48 mm or even 52 mm in size, for rattling power, if not great reliability or fuel consumption. If you go to these lengths, you will already by now have chosen one of the 6557 four-into-one exhaust pipes that have been designed for the boxer four cylinder. One thing they have in common is that they all make the motor sound a bit more purposeful than stock, and some of them don't even look too bad, either. Personally I don't like lots of chrome plating in an engine, even a modified one. It looks a bit too dressy for my tastes, although I'm not averse to the use of shiny dome nuts and just a dash of brightwork in appropriate places.

The most important thing from an appearance point of view is to do the job neatly, and to use high quality materials. For instance, don't use two buck tubing for the pump to carb hook-up after you've blown thousands on your hot engine. The art of carrying out a successful conversion lies in the attention to detail, in the workmanship as well as in the planning of the conversion.

To plan a successful conversion you have to have a good understanding of what you are after in terms of torque and power

Left
1984, the Baja 500 race in the Mojave desert; beefed-up VW mechanicals and a rather attractive body – though it's fibreglass of course

curves, driveability or revability. Generally speaking, the quickest way to more performance is to increase the capacity, despite what adverts for exhaust systems or spark intensifiers may tell you. Using a wild cam is a great thing to tell your friends about, but unless you are really focussed on living at 7,000 revs and above (remember a stock Beetle lives at about 4,500 maximum) you shouldn't go for a really way-out lobe profile.

There are some people who have levered in wild cams, hot exhausts, big valves, stroked cranks and big bore pots and the thing still doesn't come on song. More than anything else, it is important to understand the engine as a whole entity and get the various parts working together. This means that when it comes to installing big-valved heads, carbs, cams and the like, you should get an expert who's been there to advise you on the best combinations of set-up. Gas flow patterns from carb through ports, combustion chamber and exhaust are quite complex little waves to understand, and this needs careful planning if you don't want to belch and stumble your way along with a mill that never really clears out. Even a well-sorted big-carbed, hot-cammed motor can be a real pain on the streets as it fails to make useable power beneath 2,500 rpm. There again, there are some wild Vee-Dub motors I've tried that are quite streetable and yet will turn quarter miles in the 14 second bracket. They may need tuning every second day, but I know people who run such cars, so if a conversion is properly done it doesn't have to be unreliable.

Nevertheless, we should face a few facts of life. No matter how well you've balanced the motor, how refined your induction system, revs kill a motor faster than anything else. There is nothing more satisfying than winding up an incongruous-looking, but serious horse-making machine to a heady rev ceiling if it still feels sweet at those revs. But there's a price for everything, and if you can live with a high-torque number rather than a screamer and keep those revs down, your motor will probably last you until the next century.

Left

If it's more ponies you are after, there are dozens of firms to cater to your needs. This one features twin dual-throats, trick cam, crank, big bore barrels, large valve heads and lots of chrome!

Karmann Today

The name Karmann will probably be forever associated with the Type 1 Volkswagen 'special' launched in 1955. Yet hard-core motoring enthusiasts will know that Karmann has been responsible for coach-building the bodies of a whole range of classic cars throughout the century, and still do so today. From special-bodied DKWs, through Porsches, to the amazing Volkswagen Corrado coupés and the latest Golf cabriolets, the people at Karmann have been the unsung heroes of countless classics over the decades.

Of course, the most commonly-known Karmann-bodied car other than the Type 1 is the Type 3 Karmann Ghia, orginally introduced in 1962. This was based on the 'square' sedan version of the Type 3 that was launched the previous year, and featured a flat-four motor with a horizontal, 'pancake' cooling fan, instead of the upright fan common to Beetle and Type 1 Ghias. In VW production parlance, this car is known

*The famous badge that launched
400,000 shapes...*

Initially launched as a 1500S, it became a 1600 later in its life-span. It was nick-named the "razor-edge" Ghia thanks to its angular styling

as the Type 343. Initially it was called the Karmann Ghia 1500 "S", although since then fans refer to the car as the 'razor-edge' Ghia, because of its sharp body creases. The Type 3 Ghia was never all that popular, even though it was a very fine motor car, probably because it was so hard to top the Segre-Boano styling of the original and the fact that the Type 1 Ghia was still in production during the years that the Type 3 Ghia was produced. A total of 45,000 Type 3 Ghias were sold between 1962 and 1969 and they were never exported to the United States. But today, quite a few have found their way Stateside, as VW-mania continues to grow.

Given the sometimes superior attitude that Porsche aficionados had to the Karmann Ghia, it may come as a surprise to many Porsche fans to realise that Karmann in fact built a run of close to 2,000 hardtop versions of the Porsche 356 B in the early 1960s. This car carries a

unique Karmann badge with a Porsche logo superimposed upon it, mounted in a similar position to the Karmann Ghia badge, on the front fender. The Porsche 912 and 911 models also received the Karmann build quality in the late 1960s as Porsche themselves struggled to cope with demand for the car.

Apart from doing numerous special bodies and design studies for firms as diverse as AMC (American Motors Corporation) and Ford, Karmann also produced some classic BMWs over the years. The BMW 2000 CS coupé of 1965 is one of these that stands out, with period-piece slivers of metal to serve as the roof pillars and an amazingly spacious interior feel thanks to generous glass usage that was years ahead of its time. Karmann built many thousands of these bodies for the Munich-based firm. The 3.0 CS followed this vehicle in the '70s, also with the Karmann build, the firm using its Rheine factory to produce some 30,000 of these cars. BMW Motorsport immortalised the vehicle by

Above
Karmann built thousands of these beautiful BMW 3.0 CSL coupés. The yellow car features the famous racing "Batmobile" aerodynamic aids

Left
Three generations of Karmann-built cabriolets: the legendary Beetle, the second Golf version and the latest Golf III cabriolet

fitting bizarre wings and spoilers for race-track exploits, earning the nick-name 'Batmobile' for the track versions of the 3.0 CS. The svelte 6-Series coupés continued BMW's association with Karmann from the late 1970s through the '80s, the Rheine factory producing close to 90,000 of these examples for BMW, many of which still grace our roads today.

Ford has also had a long association with Karmann, and early Taurus specials were built by the Osnabruck concern. The most recent Fords to receive the Karmann touch were the Ford Merkur (very much like the Sierra Cosworth RS in appearance) and the sweet-looking Escort Cabriolet.

Talking of the Escort, the Brazilian arm of Karmann, Karmann-Ghia do Brasil Ltda, is currently building topless versions of the Ford Escort XR3, through an agreement with Auto Latina, the joint venture of VW and Ford operating in Brazil. A fact one might not normally consider when totting up total Karmann Ghia production is that from 1960 onwards the

Above
The latest incarnation of the Karmann Ghia? Karmann builds this stunning coupé for Volkswagen that is true to the original formula. A production Volkswagen in a dress suit, with improved handling and performance. This is the VR6-engined version of the latest Corrado

Right
Karmann was the logical coach-building choice for the latest Golf III in topless guise

Brazilian plant near Sao Paulo built a total of 23,577 Type I coupés. Estimates of total production vary according to source. Some Europeans sources put the total at 364,000, a figure that includes the number of cabriolets built. Karmann's published figures state that 362,000 coupés were built and 80,881 cabriolets. This figure ties in more closely with the more specific U.S. figures of 365,912 coupés, and 79,326 convertibles built between 1955 and 1974. Of course, Volkswagen dominated attention at the Osnabruck plant, and the Beetle cabriolet continued in production at Osnabruck from 1949 through until the 1980s, with production figures reaching well over the 300,000 mark before time finally ran out for the Beetle, at least at home base.

Meanwhile the Golf I cabriolet was being built in similarly impressive quantities from the mid-1970s, as was the Scirocco coupé, which has been interpreted by some as the second incarnation of the original Karmann Ghia.

In 1989, Karmann introduced a second version of the Golf Cabriolet which was in appearance halfway between the Golf I and Golf II, although it still used the basic Golf I shell. But by this stage a 'third descendant' of the Karmann Ghia was already in production, the striking VW Corrado, which today is still being produced at Osnabruck, using the potent VR6 running gear. Karmann produces the VW Golf III in cabriolet form, and the attention to detail is just as impressive as it was on the original VW-based, Italian-styled, Osnabruck-crafted Karmann Ghia that first graced the road in the second half of 1955.

Right
Karmann cabrio for the future? This Volkswagen concept vehicle, launched at Geneva Motor Show in early 1994, drew favourable comment

Colour Scheming

The following are the paint and upholstery combinations offered on Karmann Ghias from 1956 until the 1971 model year. The official paint codes are included and by quoting these numbers (e.g. L41 black) to a paint specialist, you should be able to have the identical colour mixed for you. A paint systems specialist firm, such as Spies Hecker, will have cross references that will able to translate this code number into an equivalent produced by their firm, and there are other firms that will be able to do the same. Contact your nearest Karmann specialist for advice,

or if this is impossible with your being geographically challenged, VW dealers with long memories or stocks of old workshop manuals and dealer bulletins should also be able to help.

From January 1958 to July 1960 Volkswagen offered a separate set of colour options for the convertible models. From August 1960 (the 1961 model year), the cabriolets and coupés shared similar colour charts. Depending on choice, customers could order combination vinyl and cloth upholstery for the seats, or plain vinyl.

January 1956 to August 1957

(Model Years 1956 and 1957)
Chassis nos 1 089 519 to 1 649 252.

CAR FINISH	UPHOLSTERY
L 41 Black	dark grey or black
L 318 Deep Green	dark green
L330 Trout Blue	grey
L376 Gazelle Beige	brown/copper red
L377 Deep brown	brown/khaki-beige

September 1957 to July 1959

(Model Years 1958 and 1959)
Chassis Nos 1 649 253 to 2 528 667

CAR FINISH	UPHOLSTERY (CLOTH)
L41 black	blue/blue-grey
L 241 bamboo	green
L 248 aero silver	green
L 337 dolphin-blue	blue/light blue
L 352 cognac	red
L 353 brilliant red	beige
L 354 cardinal red	red

August 1959 to July 1960

(Model Years 1960 and 1961)
Chassis Nos 2 528 668 to 3 192 506

CAR FINISH	UPHOLSTERY (CLOTH)
L41 black	red/true red
L 346 mango green	green/light green
L 347 seagull grey	green/light green
L 362 midnight blue	blue/green-grey
L 364 strato blue	blue/light blue
L 444 malachite green	beige/light beige
L 452 paprika red	stone-beige

August 1960 to July 1962

(Models Years 1961 and 1962)
Chassis Nos 3 192 507 to 4 846 835

CAR FINISH	UPHOLSTERY
L 41 black	red (cloth) true red (vinyl)
L 87 pearl white	red (cloth) true red (vinyl)
L 360 sea blue	cerulean blue (cloth) ice blue (vinyl)
L 384 pampas green	green (cloth) soft beige (vinyl)
L 397 lavender	silver (vinyl) silver beige (cloth)
L 398 pacific blue	turquoise (cloth) ice blue (vinyl)
L 452 paprika red	silver (cloth) silver beige (vinyl)
L 456 ruby red	silver (cloth) silver beige (vinyl)
L 469 anthracite	silver (cloth) silver beige (vinyl)
L 490 sierra beige	beige (cloth) light beige (vinyl)

August 1962 to July 1963

(Model Year 1963)
Chassis nos 4 846 836 to 5 677 118

CAR FINISH	UPHOLSTERY
L 41 black	brick red (cloth) brick red (vinyl)
L 87 pearl white	brick red (cloth) brick red (vinyl)
L 360 sea blue	cerulean blue (cloth) ice blue (vinyl)
L 398 pacific	turquoise (cloth) ice blue (vinyl)
L 456 ruby red	silver (cloth) silver beige (vinyl)
L 469 anthracite	brick red (cloth) brick red (vinyl)
L 514 emerald	silver (cloth) silver beige (vinyl)
L 532 polar blue	silver (cloth) ice blue (vinyl)
L 500 manila yellow	manila (cloth) black (vinyl)
L 571 terra brown	beige (cloth) light beige (vinyl)

August 1963 to July 1964

(Model year 1964)
Chassis Nos 5 677 119 to 6 502 399

CAR FINISH	UPHOLSTERY
L 41 black	red (cloth) brick red (vinyl)
L 87 pearl white	red (cloth) brick red (vinyl)
L360 sea blue	cerulean blue (cloth) ice blue (vinyl)
L 398 pacific	turquoise (cloth) ice blue (vinyl)
L 456 ruby red	silver (cloth) silver beige (vinyl)
L 469 anthracite	silver (cloth) silver beige (vinyl)
L 514 emerald green	silver (cloth) silver beige (vinyl)
L 532 polar blue	turquoise (cloth) ice blue (vinyl)
L 560 manila yellow	manila (cloth) black (vinyl)
L 571 terra brown	beige (cloth) light beige (vinyl)

August 1964 to July 1965

(Model Year 1965)
Chassis Nos 145 000 001 to 145 999 000

CAR FINISH	UPHOLSTERY
L 283 bermuda	marine (cloth) aero blue (vinyl)
L 360 sea blue	silver (cloth) aero grey (vinyl)
L 544 roulette green	beige (cloth) aero beige (vinyl)
L 553 henna red	slate (cloth) aero black (vinyl)
L 554 cherry red	slate (cloth) aero black (vinyl)
L560 manila yellow	slate (cloth) aero black (vinyl)
L 568 sea sand beige	brown (cloth) aero brown (vinyl)
L 582 arcona white	beige (cloth) aero beige (vinyl)
L 594 smoke grey	silver (cloth) aero grey (vinyl)
L 595 fontana grey	slate (cloth) aero black (vinyl)

August 1965 to July 1966

(Model Year 1966)
Chassis Nos 146 000 001 to 146 1021 300

CAR FINISH	UPHOLSTERY
L 41 black	silver (cloth) platinum (vinyl)
L 285 bermuda	azure pepita (cloth) black (vinyl)
L 360 sea blue	silver (cloth) platinum (vinyl)
L 544 roulette green	silver (cloth) platinum (vinyl)
L 553 henna red	silver (cloth) platinum (vinyl)
L 554 cherry red	silver (cloth) platinum (vinyl)
L 560 manila yellow	silver/black (cloth) black (vinyl)
L 568 sea sand	teak pepita (cloth) black (vinyl)
L 582 arcona white	teak pepita (cloth) pigalle (vinyl)
L 282 lotus white	teak papita (cloth) pigalle (vinyl)

August 1966 to July 1967

(Model year 1967)
Chassis Nos 147 000 001 to 147 999 000

CAR FINISH	UPHOLSTERY
L 41 black	indian red (vinyl only)
L 283 bermuda	blue (cloth) black (vinyl)
L 282 lotus white	khaki brown (cloth) khaki brown (vinyl)
L 10K castilian yellow	platinum (cloth) black (vinyl)
L 50K neptune blue	platinum (cloth) black (vinyl)
L 70K vulcan grey	khaki brown (cloth) light sand (vinyl)

August 1967 to July 1968

(Model year 1968)
Chassis nos 148 000 001 to 148 999 000

CAR FINISH	UPHOLSTERY
L 30K velour red	dogtooth platinum (cloth) black (vinyl)
L 041 black	dogtooth khaki (cloth) indian red (vinyl)
L 50 regatta blue	dogtooth platinum (cloth) black (vinyl)
L 61K pine green	dogtooth khaki (cloth) khaki (vinyl)
L 70F chinchilla	dogtooth khaki (cloth) khaki (vinyl)
L 80 gobi beige	dogtooth khaki (cloth) khaki (vinyl)
L 282 lotus white	dogtooth platinum (cloth) red (vinyl)
L 288 bermuda	dogtooth platinum (cloth) black (vinyl)
L 554 cherry red	dogtooth platinum (cloth) black (vinyl)

August 1968 to July 1969

(Model year 1969)
Chassis Nos 149 000 001 to 149 1200 000

CAR FINISH	UPHOLSTERY
L 11K oriole yellow	dogtooth platinum (c) khaki (v)
L 31K sunset	dogtooth platinum (c) sand (v)
L 51K chrome blue	dogtooth platinum (c) black (v)
L 62K cypress green	dogtooth khaki (c) sand (v)
L 90C toga white	dogtooth platinum (c) black (v)
L 554 cherry red	dogtooth platinum (c) sand (v)

August 1969 to July 1970

(Model Year 1970)
Chassis Nos 140 2000 001 to 140 21200 000

CAR FINISH	UPHOLSTERY
10 E pampas yellow	dogtooth platinum (c) khaki (v)
L 20E amber	dogtooth platinum (c) sand (v)
L 30E bahra red	dogtooth platinum (c) sand (v)
L 41 black	dogtooth platinum (c) sand (v)
L 51 albert blue	dogtooth platinum (c) sand (v)
L 52 pastel blue	dogtooth platinum (c) sand (v)
L 60E Irish green	dogtooth platinum (c) sand (v)
L 80E light ivory	dogtooth platinum (c) black (v)

August 1970 –

(Model year 1971–)
From Chassis No 141 2000 001

CAR FINISH	UPHOLSTERY
L 11E lemon yellow	cord black (c) black (v)
L 20E amber	cord black (c) black (v)
L 21E blood orange	cord black (c) black (v)
L 30E bahra red	cord black (c) black (v)
L 41E black	cord black (c) black (v)
L 50E adria blue	cord black (c) black (v)
L 60E Irish green	cord black (c) black (v)
L 63K willow green	cord black (c) black (v)
L 80E light ivory	cord black (c) black (v)
L 96D silver metallic	cord black (c) black (v)
L 96E gemeni metallic	cord black (c) black (v)
L 97G gold metallic	cord black (c) black (v)

NOTES:
This paint colour-upholstery list is given as a guide to restorers who are
keen to return their cars to original. Note that mono tones and two tones
were available for most years, with white or black being the most common
colour for the roof. However, although all body paint options are listed,
only the primary upholstery options are given, in the interests of keeping a
workable list. For example, for the 1971 model year on, Karmann offered
two additional cloth finishes (cord leather black and palisander cord) on all
the colours listed, and two additional vinyls (palisander and leather beige),
also available on all 12 listed body colours. On earlier years, numerous
other upholstery options were available, but in different combinations. For
instance, in the 1968 model year, indian red vinyl was offered as an option
with the bermuda L 288 bodypaint colour. Only the most common
combinations are given, although it should be noted that black vinyl was an
option common to many interiors from the 1964 model year onwards.

The Numbers Game

A guide to chassis numbers, production figures, specifications and other Karmann-specific left-brain challenges. The following list is compiled according to Model Year and not calendar year. Note that Karmann announced their new models for the following year in August. In others words, a 1965 model Karmann Ghia was produced from August 1, 1964 until July 31, 1965. For this reason there is no listing for a 1955 Ghia.

The first model year was 1956, as the Karmann Ghia made its official debut in September 1955 at the Frankfurt Auto Show. However, the press were given a preview on July 14, 1955, with production starting on August 1 of that year. The car did not go on sale until after the show, and by December of 1955, the Osnabruck works had signed off a total of 1,282 "1956" Karmann Ghias.

YEAR	CHASSIS NOS		
1956	1060 930	to	1394 119
1957	1394 420	to	1774 680
1958	1774 681	to	2226 206
1959	2226 207	to	2528 668
1960	2528 660	to	3192 507
1961	3192 508	to	4010 995
1962	4010 996	to	4840 8336
1963	4840 837	to	5677 119
1964	5677 120	to	6502 399
1965	145 000 001	to	145 999 000
1966	146 000 001	to	146 1021 300
1967	147 000 001	to	147 999 001
1968	148 000 001	to	148 1016 100
1969	149 000 001	to	149 1200 000
1970	140 2000 001	to	140 3100 000
1971	141 2000 001	to	141 3200 000
1972	142 2000 001	to	142 3200 000
1973	143 2000 001	to	143 3200 001
1974	144 2000 001	to	144 2999 000

A world-wide total of 365,912 Type 1 (or Type 14, if you are talking VW production line lingo) Karmann Ghia coupés were produced, as well as 79,326 convertibles; sold all over the world, although American sales represent well over 60 per cent of the total production. The most rare model in terms of production numbers is the 1973 convertible and the most common model is the 1970 coupé. However, it figures that by 1994 standards, a 1958 cabriolet has to be the rarest of all, as relatively fewer of these survive than the run-out cabriolet models of the 1970s. World-wide production figures ran at an average of 24,000 units a year, with a high in the 1969 calendar year (not model year, note) of 34 000 units.

GENERAL SPECIFICATIONS

1955 Model

Dimensions:

Overall length	4140 mm
Overall width	1630 mm
Overall height	1325 mm
Wheelbase.	2400 mm
Front track.	1290 mm
Rear track	1250 mm
Ground clearance	172 mm
Wheel size	4J by 15
Tyre size	5.60 X 15

Suspension:

Front: king pin-link pin, transverse torsion bars

Rear: swing axles, transverse torsion bars

Steering: worm and nut (2.4 turns, lock-to-lock)

Dry weight: 790 kg

Capacities:

Fuel tank:. 40 litres (8.8 Imp gall, 10,6 U.S. gall)

Engine oil: 2,5 litres (4,4 Imp pints, 5.3 U.S. pints)

Transmission Oil: 2,5 litres (4.4 Imp pints, 5.3 U.S. pints)

CALENDAR YEAR WORLD-WIDE PRODUCTION

YEAR	COUPE	CABRIOLET	YEAR	COUPE	CABRIOLET
1955	1,282		1965	28,387	5,326
1956	11,555		1966	23,387	5,395
1957	15,369	105	1967	19,406	4,183
1958	14,515	4,392	1968	24,729	5,713
1959	17,196	4,585	1969	27,834	6,504
1960	19,259	5,465	1970	24,893	6,398
1961	16,708	3,965	1971	21,133	6,565
1962	18,812	4,750	1972	12,434	2,910
1963	22,829	5,433	1973	10,462	2,555
1964	25,267	5,262	1974	7,167	———

PERFORMANCE-RELATED SPECIFICATIONS

1956 to 1959 Model Years

Output: 30 hp (DIN) at 3400 rpm
Bore and Stroke: 77 mm by 64 mm
Capacity: 1192 cc
Compression Ratio: 6.6:1
Carburettor: Solex 28 PIC
Final Drive Ratio: 4.4:1

1960 to 1965 Model Years

Output: 34 hp (DIN) at 3600 rpm
Capacity: 1192 cc
Compression ratio: 7.0:1
Carburettor: Solex 28 PICT. (From November 1963, the 28 PICT-1 was used)
Final Drive: 4.375:1

1966 Model Year

Output: 40 hp (DIN) at 4000 rpm
Bore and Stroke: 77 mm by 69 mm
Capacity: 1285 cc
Compression ratio: 7.3:1
Carburettor: Solex 30 PICT-1

1967 Model Year

Output: 44 hp (DIN) at 4000 rpm
Bore and Stroke: 83 mm by 69 mm
Capacity: 1493 cc
Compression Ratio: 7.5:1
Carburettor: Solex 30 PICT-1
Final Drive: 4.125:1

NB: the 1300 model was offered alongside the 1500 for two years.

1971 Model Year

Output: 50 hp (DIN) at 4000 rpm
Bore and Stroke: 85.5 by 69 mm
Capacity: 1584 cc
Carburettor: Solex 30 PICT-3. (From June 1971, Solex 34 PICT-3)
Final Drive Ratio: 4.375:1

Contacts

PARTS AND RESTORATION

AMERICA

JUST GHIAS, 901 Rampart Range Road, Woodland Park, Colorado 80863.
A division of Beetle specialists Rocky Mountain Motorworks, Just Ghias supplies a vast range of specialised Ghia parts, including Hella headlamps and tail lamps, reproduction parts, NOS parts and used parts such as bumpers. They are particularly strong in the rubber seal and door panel fields.

HOUSE OF GHIA, 2626 Three Lakes Road, Albany, Oregon.
Suppliers of lots of NOS equipment for Ghias and a massive range of used and/or restored parts, in fact just about everything that has ever been featured on a Ghia in all 19 years of production. House of Ghia offer a very informative catalogue with loads of restoration tips and detailed exploded drawings.

KARMANN GHIA PARTS AND RESTORATION, PO Box 58, Moorpark California, 93020.
The staff at Karmann Ghia Parts and Restoration own 40 Ghias between them, which says something about their commitment to the cause. They restore Ghias as well as offer an almost complete range of spare parts for the cars, new, reproduction or used. The catalog they produce features factory-type exploded views of parts, of extreme value during a restoration.

J BUGS CAR AND TRUCK DEPOT, 14222 S. Prairie Avenue, Hawthorne, California 90250.
Specialist in rubber mouldings and seals for all models, upholstery, carpeting, convertible tops, maple wood bows, and frame fittings.

VW RESTORATION PARTS, Box 31555 Broad Street Complex, Richmond, Virginia 23294.
This Virginia company offers a full range of accessories, beauty rims, as well as restoration parts for Ghias.

CALIFORNIA PACIFIC, 2040 Oceanside Boulevard, Oceanside, California 92054.
This firm specialises in carpet kits, rubber and vinyl tops in both vinyl and Haartz Stayfast cloth.

SEW FINE 5815 QW 6th Avenue, 2-C Lakewood, Colorado
Convertible top experts, offering outers, headliners, and frame bow replacements. They also do upholstery replacement kits in original and far-out custom styles.

WEST COAST METRIC, 24002 Frampton Avenue, #VT, Harbor City, California 90710.
Perhaps the best reputation in providing German replacement and reproduction parts such as wiring looms, convertible tops, window rubber and aluminium mouldings.

KOCH'S STEERING WHEEL RESTORATION PO Box 784 Newhall, California 91321.
This firm provides NOS items and restores exhausted steering wheels, including those excruciatingly rare 1958 and 1959 Ghia-only wheels. They offer a host of VW-wheel-related items such as badges, horn/hooter rings, etc.

UK

KARMANN CLASSICS, 96-98 Northease Drive, Hove, Sussex BN3 8LH.
This is one of the premier Ghia specialists in Britain. Among a host of other spares, they offer genuine replacement body panels for Ghias, as well as top quality repro replacement panels.

KARMANN KONNECTION, 4-6 High Street, A13, Hadleigh, Essex, SS7, 2PB.
This is the most famous Ghia restoration outfit in Europe, let alone Britain, where Karmann interest is at fever pitch. Lights, rubbers, bumpers, badges and body repair panels are on offer with lots of other goodies.

GERMAN CAR COMPANY, Britavia House, Southend Airport, Southend on Sea, Essex SS2 6YU.
Specialists in accessories for Type 1 VWs, as well as rubber seals for Ghias. A good place to go to if you are thinking of a Cal-look Ghia.

SOUTH AFRICA

BEETLE SPARES, PO Box 81 Viljoensdrift, 9580. Tel (016) 57 1578.
Manned by Nico and Maya Rudolph, this is a good source for tail lights and body panels.

MAGAZINES

VW TRENDS.
Published in the USA by McMullen and Yee of Placentia Avenue, Placentia, California 92670.
This well-presented monthly magazine of around 120 pages is for the young or young-at-heart VW fan, with special leanings to Cal-look Bugs and Ghias. Also carries the odd concise feature on Ghias or Ghia restoration.

DUNE BUGGIES AND HOT VWS
Published by Wright Publishing Co of P O Box 2260 Costa Mesa.
Perhaps the only real weakness of this 150 page or so magazine is its cover, which deserves to be either printed on thicker paper or perfect bound so it won't shear off. Most VW freaks collect this one as THE source, since it has been around since the early 1970s and has been largely responsible or keeping the air-cooled flame of interest alive. Apart from some great feature pics, the articles are for the slightly more technically-orientated VW lover. A great source for DIY articles.

VOLKSWORLD
Published by Link House Magazines of Dingwall Avenue, Croydon, CR9 2TA, England.
A classy mag with a strong leaning towards restoration, it carries a good article on Ghias every other month or so.

VW MOTORING
This is probably the world's oldest surviving VW-specific mag, having started out life as VW Safer Motoring in the early 1960s. The accent is on serious DIY and serious VW motoring, with the odd well-detailed, if rather formal Ghia article featured.

CLUBS

KARMANN GHIA OWNERS' CLUB OF GREAT BRITAIN 47 Toton Lane, Stapleford, Nottingham, NG9 7HB, United Kingdom

'56 TO '59 KARMANN GHIA REGISTRY Jeffrey P Lipnichan, 961 Village Road, Lancaster, Pennsylvania 17602 USA.

KARMANN GHIA AND BEETLE CLUB OF SOUTH AFRICA C/O M van Zyl, Reid Street 30A, Westdene, Bloemfontein 9301 South Africa.